Spiritual Disciplines
for Children

Vernie Schorr Love

All Scripture quotations, unless otherwise indicated, are taken from the HOLY BIBLE, NEW INTERNATIONAL VERSION®. Copyright © 1973, 1978, 1984 International Bible Society. Used by permission of Zondervan. All rights reserved. Other versions used include: New Revised Standard Version Bible, (NRSV), copyright © 1989 National Council of the Churches of Christ in the United States of America. Used by permission. All rights reserved. Scripture quotations marked NLT are taken from the Holy Bible, New Living Translation, copyright 1996, 2004. Used by permission of Tyndale House Publishers, Inc., Wheaton, Illinois 60189. All rights reserved. Scripture taken from *The Message* (MSG). Copyright © 1993, 1994, 1995, 1996, 2000, 2001, 2002. Used by permission of NavPress Publishing Group. Scriptures quoted from the *International Children's Bible, New Century Version,* copyright © 1983, 1986, 1988 by Word Publishing, Dallas, Texas, 75039 (marked ICB). Used by permission.

Cover design: Kathryn Baker Schorr
Cover art: *Boys in a Dory* (detail) by Winslow Homer, 1880

Printed in the United States of America

For permission to use material, contact:

Vernie Schorr Love
Character Choice
408 Lone Eagle Pt.
Lafayette, Colorado 80026
303.419.8811
vschorr@characterchoice.org

ISBN: 0-615620-87-6
ISBN 13: 978-0615620879

Visit www.characterchoice.org to order additional copies.

Spiritual Disciplines
for Children

*A Guide to a Deeper Spiritual Life
for You and Your Children*

Vernie Schorr Love

Inspired By Richard J. Foster's *Celebration of Discipline*

To the parents, teachers, and coaches whose deep love and concern for the spiritual life of children has connected them to the training and ministry of Character Choice. These individuals continue to practice and train both adults and children to reach their communities with the hope of Christ. As they continue my hope is that, through this resource, they may go farther in the amazing adventure of spiritual and character formation in themselves, their families, and their children. I am so grateful for their stories, and I continue to learn from them. They are my heroes and heroines.

Contents

Acknowledgments

My deep gratitude goes to the many persons who have helped me along the way.

To my family, especially my husband, Roger, for patience, encouragement, love, and never allowing me to quit.

To Bob Hunt, who believed this book needed to be written and convinced me to be the writer.

To Tom Forbes, Sharon Floyd, Bishop Sterling Lands, and Kathy and Tom Palmer, my exceptional board.

To Richard Foster, Chris Webb, and Lyle SmithGraybeal, for their support and guidance.

To Karen Roberts, my faithful editor and close friend. She is always available, always encouraging me to move from good to great.

To my reviewers, Barbara Bingham, Lacy Borgo, Bob Dunshee, Amy Fenton Lee, Jennifer Love, Rev. Christopher Sze Ho Lui, Traci Mancino, Lee Ann Nickerson, Sherrie Shackel-Dorren, Lyle SmithGraybeal, Amy Trent, Sibyl Towner, and Omer Troyer.

To my ministry partners, whose prayers and support for this book kept me going—without you I would never have finished.

To the Creator of all, my Helper and Guide, whose power, grace, and love never fail.

Introduction

Trust in the Lord with all your heart and lean not on your own understanding; in all your ways acknowledge him, and he will make your paths straight.

Proverbs 3:5–6

I love to be around children. I have been relating to children as a teacher, parent, grandparent, and friend for the past forty years. My profound discovery is that children have a deep need in their lives to have a sense of belonging, worth, and competence. This discovery has created a passion in me. That passion is to give children the opportunity to know, love, and serve the Lord Jesus of the Bible and become people who live out and reflect God's ways and character. To do so not only fills their deep need but also fulfills my lifelong call as an advocate for children.

> Children have a deep need in their lives to have a sense of belonging, worth, and competence.

Why Spiritual Disciplines For Children?

Reaching children with the truth that Jesus loves them has in recent years become an industry of entertainment with HD big screens and theme rooms that would make Hollywood proud. One may argue that the children enjoy and love these fun-filled times. And they do. But what about the spiritual health of these children? Entertainment experiences, regardless of the level of their spiritual focus, are not enough to intentionally form the spiritual life of children and grow their personal, intimate relationship with God and His Son Jesus.

George Barna, in his book *Transforming Children Into Spiritual Champions*, relates that "every dimension of a person's experience hinges on his or her moral and spiritual condition."[1] He goes on to describe the challenge that we face as people who guide children.

The statistics pertaining to the spiritual life and experience of children are rather alarming. Given the trends indicating that your spiritual condition by the age of 13 is a strong predictor of your spiritual profile as an adult, it seems clear that a deep and robust spiritual life demands intentional and strategic spiritual nurturing during the early childhood and adolescent years.

Consider the facts. People are much more likely to accept Christ as their Savior when they are young. Absorption of biblical information and principles typically peaks during the preteen years. Beliefs and attitudes about the viability and value of church participation form early in life. Habits related to the practice of one's faith develop when one is young and change surprisingly little over time.

Although we spend roughly 68 times more money per capita on caring for the average felon than on a church's ministry to a spiritually hungry child and we spend substantially more on church buildings and maintenance than on raising up spiritual champions among our progeny, I don't believe the central issue is finance. More than anything, it is an issue of understanding the incredible importance of developing strong, spiritual foundations early and reinforcing those foundations as the child ages.[2]

The battle we are engaged in for children is spiritual. The battlefield is the spirit, character, and minds of our children, which are being filled to a great extent by commercial television, film, and music industries that convey the view that the measure of success in society is the accumulation of material wealth and the frequency of experiences of sensual pleasure and adrenaline rushes. Our cultures are often more successful at developing children to be self-indulgent than at nurturing them in the pursuit of a spiritual life with God that gives meaning, purpose, and joy to life.

In the midst of this struggle, I am encouraged to witness children being inspired to greater ideals and looking for ways to live their lives for good and for the good of others. I find children searching for a deeper relationship with God and a desire to prioritize and nurture their spiritual life. When given the opportunity to understand and practice spiritual disciplines such as "thinking about God, listening, and hearing God's voice" (meditation) or habitually giving away two items when purchasing or acquiring one (simplicity), children rise to the adventure.

Nothing is more influential or more detrimental in the spiritual life of children than the power of quiet example. Children need to see parents, grandparents, relatives, teachers, coaches, and others obediently living out the ways and character of

> Nothing is more influential or more detrimental in the spiritual life of children than the power of quiet example.

God as demonstrated in the life of Christ. However, since culture bombards them with much of the opposite message, we must add to our quiet example intentional activities that guide them in life with God. And that is what this book is about.

It is my hope that the ideas and concepts in the following pages give you the understanding and methods to first consider your *spiritual alignment* and the personal practice of *spiritual disciplines* in your life. Then, as you practice and model your relationship with God and these disciplines, you become intentional in choosing ways to guide children in spiritual practices—ways that result in lifelong patterns and habits that lead children to a deeper, intimate relationship and life with God and His Son Jesus.

Spiritual Alignment

The term *spiritual formation* used in this book refers to the fact that all human beings have a spiritual component to their existence. It does not mean, however, that they currently have a personal relationship with God through Jesus Christ, which is an intimate, personal decision. *Godly spiritual formation* is the formation of spirit, character, and mind toward Christ. The result is a personal, vertical relationship with God that continues to mature in consistent obedience throughout life.

Relationships are two-way, and they require a connection. The connection "aligns" those in the relationship in one way or another. The cross of Christ gives us a concrete picture of our relationship alignments—vertical with God and horizontal with each other.

A vital, personal relationship with Christ precedes and fully integrates with all true spiritual and character formation. The relationship is an internal relationship with God through Jesus by faith that begins with God coming down to us. We then have the choice to accept this God initiated relationship, surrender self, and follow Him, choosing obedience to Him before self. This relationship is vertical and internal. This relationship is Lordship! Jesus is Master. We serve Him. His role is Creator and Sustainer and Lord of all. He is the ultimate authority. Our role is to be obedient to Him as the ultimate authority (Colossians 3:2 "Set your minds on things above").

When the personal vertical relationship with God is intimate and constant, our horizontal relationships and friendships with others become real and authentic. The vertical relationship must be kept straight. Our life with God needs to stay in alignment vertically, and then we are able to live out horizontally His ways and character in our everyday, walk-around lives.

"A personal relationship with one another reflects a vertical relationship with God. We can refer to this as a horizontal relationship with one another. As the vertical relationship is totally dependent upon one's faith in God, the horizontal relationship with one another is totally dependent upon one's obedience to the word and will of God."[3]

Horizontal relationships are a reflection of our obedience to God. They reflect Christ's likeness in three fundamental aspects of our being: our beliefs that drive

xiv   Spiritual Disciplines for Children

our behavior, our attitudes that drive our actions, and our character that drives our conduct (Romans 12:9). For Christ followers who guide children, there is no more critical need than to establish this horizontal relationship with children.

Spiritual disciplines are tools that we use for improving our life with God and our representation of God. Spiritual disciplines are the means by which we refine and improve what we believe in about God and our life with God. Spiritual disciplines help us to be partakers of the divine nature.

In order for you to be an authentic, genuine, effective guide for children, you need to have a genuine vertical relationship with God and practice and model the spiritual discipline tools consistently in your own life.

Intentional Formation

Spiritual and character formation takes place intentionally or unintentionally. It is imperative, therefore, for us to intentionally guide children in godly spiritual and character practices and patterns at the earliest possible age.

It is imperative for us to guide children intentionally in godly spiritual and character practices and patterns at the earliest possible age.

In his book *Celebration of Discipline,* Richard Foster identifies twelve disciplines that, when practiced in our ordinary lives, nurture spiritual maturity and deepen our connection with God. Foster's twelve spiritual disciplines are: meditation, prayer, fasting, study, simplicity, solitude, submission, service, confession, worship, guidance, and celebration. God has ordained these disciplines, says Foster, as the means by which we place ourselves where God can bless us.

In the context of our life with God, the word *discipline* refers to the intentional attitude and conduct choices that become firmly established spiritual practices and lifelong patterns and habits in our lives. The goal of these spiritual practices, patterns, and habits is to put us in the place where the Holy Spirit is able to do God's inner transformation of our spirit, mind, and character.

The intentional, personal, and habitual practice of spiritual disciplines invites God's Spirit to change us, to build His character in us, to make us more like His Son Jesus, and to reveal how to live our lives with God and with others.

The intentional, personal, and habitual practice of spiritual disciplines invites God's Spirit to change us, to build His character in us, to make us more like His Son Jesus, and to reveal how to live our lives with God and with others. The result is that we become people who reflect God's character and the ways of Jesus in our daily, walk-around lives.

The practice of spiritual disciplines enables us to know God more fully and experience Him more continuously in our everyday lives. Spiritual disciplines replace destructive patterns of thought, belief, attitudes, and conduct with constructive patterns of thought, belief, attitudes, and conduct. Or in other words, spiritual disciplines create life-giving practices that become lifelong patterns and habits.

> The task for us as people who guide children is to cast the practice of spiritual disciplines into concrete experiences for our children.

The task for us as people who guide children is to cast the practice of spiritual disciplines into concrete experiences for our children. We need to become capable interpreters of God's book the Bible, His ways, and His character for them by translating God's ways and character into children's language and experiences.

Spiritual disciplines are not a subject that we can just teach to children. They are practices, patterns, and habits that we also must model and live out, first in our personal life, and then in community with the children God has placed in our lives.

A word about patterns and habits. They are, quite simply, approaches and skills that become "patterns" and "habits" to ensure that a person "habitually" employs chosen patterns and habits in everyday life. Habits or patterns for children might include hanging up clothes, putting toys or video equipment away, and consistently using the words *please* and *thank you*. Habits or patterns for spiritual disciplines might include talking to God every day and making simpler choices.

Sterling Lands, in his book *The Main Ingredient*, tells us, "Habits are powerful factors in our lives. Because they are consistent, often unconscious patterns, they constantly express our character and produce our effectiveness or ineffectiveness."[4]

The Importance Of A Biblical Set Of Beliefs

Many people holding many different spiritual beliefs would agree that there is a need for spiritual disciplines. Some may seek to grasp and employ the concepts presented in this book even though they have another god or concept of God as a base for spiritual development. For this reason, a biblical set of beliefs is crucial for spiritual and character formation in the image of God and His Son Jesus.

A *set of beliefs*, sometimes called a worldview, can be defined as a set of presuppositions (or assumptions) that are held consciously or subconsciously about the basic makeup of the world. Beliefs are built or formed by significant adults, by cultures, and by life experiences. Some beliefs within a set of beliefs can be partially true or false (Santa Claus, the Easter Bunny).

A *biblical set of beliefs* is *radically* different from other sets of beliefs. Its formation starts with people who search for and deserve an honest answer. A biblical set of beliefs asks people to use their minds to discover the truth of the universe and conclude that what the Bible talks about is true:

- There is an eternal Person who feels and thinks.

- This person is God, who made energy and who made human beings in His image.

- God is a personal creator. He created each of us individually; therefore, there is a purpose to our individual existence.

- We live in a moral universe. Right and wrong are clearly defined. They are not imposed by power. They have something to do with the kind of world God has made. And to break the laws of right and wrong is not merely to violate God's attitudes and character. It is to do something utterly destructive and foolish in the kind of world we live in.

- We live in a rational, ordered universe. The earth is an orderly place. The sun continues to give us light for each day, and the moon follows its twenty-eight day cycle. The earth stays on its axis and continues to rotate so that we have day and night. The earth continues to go around the sun every year, which gives us seasons. This orderliness testifies to God's authority.

This biblical set of beliefs holds the truth that the Bible relates to all of life. This truth permeates our lives and the lives of our children from the earliest ages and continues as an ongoing, lifelong process.

This Resource

Spiritual disciplines (practices, patterns, and habits) for followers of Jesus are meant to become an intrinsic part of our lives, not some means to new or exciting spiritual mountaintop experiences. The purpose of personally pursuing them is to allow God's Holy Spirit to accomplish God's transforming work *in us*. The purpose of guiding children in the practice of spiritual disciplines is to allow God's Holy Spirit to accomplish God's transforming work *in them* at the earliest ages. This resource is designed to help you achieve both purposes.

Each chapter of this resource focuses on one spiritual discipline, written to engage you personally in ways to incorporate the discipline into your life as well as ways to guide children in age-appropriate practices of the discipline. The first five disciplines, presented in chapters 1 through 5, are personal and inward disciplines; the seven that follow, presented in chapters 6 through 12, are outward disciplines.

Each chapter includes

- "child friendly wording" for the spiritual discipline

- an explanation of the spiritual discipline for Christ followers

- Scriptures that describe and fortify the concept and use of the spiritual discipline

- a focused discussion on God's character that links the practice of the spiritual discipline with one or more aspects of God's character (see the Appendix)

- reflection questions and response suggestions to help you make the most of the chapter materials in your life

- activities and guided conversations for beginning the practice of the spiritual discipline with children

The "Focus on God's Character" section connects your understanding and practice of the discipline to one or more aspects of God's character being formed by God's Spirit in you and your children. The "Ways for You to Practice and Model" section is your opportunity to both reflect on and respond to the content of the chapter, applying it personally for the purpose of growing your life with God.

At the end of each chapter, I have included activities with guided conversation to enable children to practice each spiritual discipline. The activities include but are not limited to art, music, drama, written and oral communication, science, and games. Reinforcement pages that are reproducible have been provided in some but not all chapters.

One final but important comment about the content in this resource. The concrete nature of the ideas and activities presented here are especially helpful for relating difficult concepts to children who learn in unconventional means. I encourage you to try them with children with special needs.

Guided Conversation

The importance of *guided conversation* cannot be overemphasized. Guided conversation makes possible the building of good relationships, the discovery of a child's knowledge, and opportunities to guide learners' beliefs, attitudes, and understanding. Guided conversation also enables affirming children's discernment about God's presence and direction.

Keep in mind that words have tremendous power. The words we use and the way we guide conversation greatly impact spiritual and character formation in children, their families, and communities.

Guided conversation makes it possible to explore openly and freely children's deepest questions about their personal lives, their families, their friends, their school, and their play experiences. In my years of serving children and facilitating the learning of others who serve children, I have found that some adults consider opening this conversation avenue a bit of a threat. Perhaps it is because they have come to believe that they must have all the answers to children's questions.

When you do not know how to answer a child's question, simply say, "I don't know the answer to your question. Let's begin to pray and research to find some information together." In order to offer children a fuller experience of life with God, it is our responsibility to draw out, in everyday, walk-around experiences, an understanding of God and God's desires for the people He created.

Guided conversation creates the opportunity to model spiritual disciplines and character virtues. See the Appendix for more ideas, skills, and activities to enhance your use of guided conversation.

An Indispensable Framework Of How Children Think And Learn

The most effective spiritual and character formation in children occurs when those who guide children do so from what I consider to be an indispensible framework of how children think and learn. This framework includes (1) essential information about the five areas of child development, (2) basic skills to guide children's clear understanding of biblical beliefs and spiritual disciplines, and (3) six challenges related to how children think and learn. Throughout this book you will see reminders of this framework as it applies to discussions about guiding children in their understanding and practice of the spiritual disciplines.

An extended section titled "An Indispensable Framework of How Children Think and Learn" is in the Appendix of this book. It includes examples to increase your understanding of interactions with children concerning spiritual and character formation. I strongly recommend the often reading of this material as you guide your children in the practice of these spiritual disciplines.

The Continuing Journey

This book is my way of helping you in your continuing journey to form spiritual disciplines in your life and in your children's lives. The forming does not necessarily occur in the order presented in these pages, but formation continues as you explore each of the twelve disciplines in whichever order you choose. When your first reading and application of the materials in this resource is completed, I encourage you to start all over, because the disciplines are never mastered. Instead, they are approached and understood in ever more maturing ways, in all the different areas and stages of development, throughout life.

> The disciplines are never mastered. Instead, they are approached and understood in ever more maturing ways.

Some of you may expect to read through this resource quickly, looking for quick answers, thinking you will go back to absorb and apply them more fully in a second reading of it. I encourage you to remember that the condition of the spiritual life of parents and teachers is closely connected to that of the children they serve. My suggestion is that you set aside the time you need in your first reading to begin to practice and live out each discipline. At the same time, begin to model and guide children in each discipline by using the suggested activities.

Keep in mind always that the greatest challenges of our time are not technological or even political or economic, because the challenges in these areas, glaring as they may be, are largely traceable back to something else. The greatest challenges are building spirit and character that reflect God's ways and character in us and in the next generations. History tells us that advanced cultures declined in the past because of decline and deterioration of moral and spiritual standards. Unless we intentionally build spirit and character that reflect God's ways and character in children, our present cultures will turn away from God. It is for these reasons that it is so important for you, the reader, to persevere in the cultivation and practice of these spiritual disciplines in both you and your children.

Chapter One

The Practice of Meditation—
Think, Listen, and Hear

*Think over what I say, for the Lord will give you understanding
in all things.*

2 Timothy 2:7, *The Renovaré Spiritual Formation Bible,* NRSV

Where there is peace and meditation, there is neither anxiety nor doubt.

St. Francis of Assisi

"Was God here before Grandma and Grandpa?" a child asked.

Thinking about God is a natural curiosity for children. Thinking is a good place to begin exploring the spiritual discipline of meditation.

Many people practice one or more forms of meditation for reasons of relaxation, physical fitness, and other belief systems. The practice of meditation described in this chapter, however, is specifically the spiritual discipline of meditation that focuses on the words and ways of God.

The Practice Of Meditation For Followers Of Jesus

Meditation gives us the opportunity to focus ourselves on God by thinking, listening, and hearing. When we think about God, we allow Him to invite us to trust Him, to enjoy His comfort, and to experience His guidance. Meditation enables us to have a rich attachment to God and, at the same time, detachment from the hurriedness, noise, and confusion around us.

Thinking is only one part of meditation. Richard Foster describes the spiritual discipline of meditation for those who follow Jesus as "the ability to hear God's voice and obey His word."[1] My child friendly wording for *meditation* is "thinking about God, listening, and hearing His voice."

> *Meditation* is thinking about God, listening, and hearing His voice.

God's people down through the ages have practiced the discipline of meditation in order to nurture a familiar, intimate relationship with Him. In words that children can understand, "a familiar, intimate relationship with God" may be called "the with-God life." I begin and continue to use the phrase "the with-God life" with children at the earliest ages to help grow in them the truth that God is with them here and now.

Many adults struggle with the practice of meditation. Had they been given the opportunity to practice thinking about God, listening, and hearing His voice as young children, their ways of meditation with God might be less of a struggle. Mark, a member of my small group of people ages 45-plus, is an example. One evening when I introduced the practice to think about God, listen, and hear His voice, Mark gently said, "Do you really hear God's voice? How do you know it is God's voice and not just your wishful thinking?"

I cited several events in the Bible when people experienced hearing God's voice, including the young child Samuel (1 Samuel 3:2–10), Jeremiah (Jeremiah 1:6–8), Gideon (Judges 6), Hosea (Hosea 1:2–5), and Jesus (Luke 3:22). "Also," I said, "modern day testimonies of God's people having this intimate relationship with God are not unusual. In my own life, I often hear God's voice in times of silence and when thinking on a verse or portion of Scripture such as Psalm 46:10, 'Be still, and know that I am God; I will be exalted among the nations, I will be exalted in the earth.'"

"I really, really want to hear God's voice," Mark replied.

Over the next several months, Mark continued to express his desire to hear God's voice and his frustration of not experiencing this connection with God even though he practiced thinking about God and listening for His voice. Then one evening he excitedly shared, "It happened. I really heard God's voice." He went on to describe what happened.

> I was riding my bike and, as usual, had my radio earphones on. About half way through my ride, I had the sense that I needed to take the earphones off and talk to God. My mind wandered and continually went to my job. I kept trying to pull it back and began to think about the insight that God had given

me this morning about being a grape on the branch. Without staying connected to the vine or Jesus, I would never become wine that can be poured out like Jesus was.

I began to think about my missionary friend Jeff. I wanted to ask him how he heard God's voice. Was it through the Scriptures, people, circumstances, the church, or God directly? Suddenly Scripture verse after Scripture verse popped into my head. And then it hit me! I wasn't "thinking" about these things or they weren't just randomly coming to mind. The Holy Spirit, in fact, was speaking to me. No loud voice or neon signs, but quiet insights. God had answered me and spoken to me. It was a day I will never forget.

The coolest thing is that He has spoken to me again on several occasions. Not always when I want, but I think when He wants. I simply long for more.

John Ortberg has wisely said that many people who think God isn't talking to them just do not realize that He is. Mark's experience with the discipline of meditation continues to increase his relationship with God. He also describes a growing awareness of becoming a person who is more compassionate, forgiving, and desiring of integrity because of his practice of meditation.

> Many people who think God isn't talking to them just do not realize that He is.

It is important to note here that although I define meditation for children as thinking about God, listening, and hearing His voice, I am not implying that these aspects of meditation are in any way sequential. We may sometimes hear God's voice when we are not intentionally listening for it. At other times we may listen and think but receive simply the comforting sense that He loves us and is with us.

Though adults may struggle with meditation, of all the spiritual disciplines, meditation seems to me to be the one that children can most easily grasp and put into practice in their daily, walk-around lives. The following sets of ideas and the "Activities and Guided Conversations for Children" at the end of this chapter may be used to guide children intentionally into the practice of meditation.

> Though adults may struggle with meditation, of all the spiritual disciplines, meditation seems to me to be the one that children can most easily grasp and put into practice in their daily, walk-around lives.

Focus On God's Character

Everyone's spirit and character are continuously being formed. The question is, what is the basis of the formation? The practice of spiritual disciplines is one basis from which character may be formed to reflect God's character. For this reason, through-out this book you will see an intentional focus on God's char-acter as part of the practice of each spiritual discipline.

Compassion
Forgiveness
Integrity
Respect
Responsibility
Initiative
Cooperation
Perseverance

Thoughts about what God is like are part of meditation, so guide children to think about God's nature and character at the earliest ages. God's character virtues include compas-sion, forgiveness, integrity, respect, responsibility, initiative, cooperation, and perseverance. You might begin your focus on God's character by guiding children to think about the virtue of compassion. Say to children, "God is a compassion-ate God. He loves all the people of the world. What are some ways God tells you that He loves you?"

> Begin to guide children to think about God's nature and character at the earliest ages.

Give children thoughts and words that tell them the way that God shows His character of compassion to the world. "God's compassion for the people of the world is so great that He sent His Son Jesus to tell them He loves every man, woman, boy, and girl." Then define the word *compassion*. "Compassion is sympathy for someone else's suffering or misfortune, together with the desire to help, and appropriate ac-tion for his or her benefit." (See the Appendix for a chart of virtues and definitions.)

Encourage children to think about asking God to teach and guide them to treat all people with equal compassion. Ask them to imagine the difference it would make in their home or at school to go through just one day asking God to help them re-spond and act as a person of compassion.

Ideas For Children To Think About God

Children enjoy thinking about God. What does He look like? Where does God live? Does Jesus live with God? Does God have to eat all His vegetables? Who made God? These questions are only a few of their creative and imaginative thoughts about God. When children ask these kinds of questions, use the occasions as teachable moments. Label their questions as a practice of meditation. "I enjoy listening to you practice meditating on God by thinking about Him and what He is like."

Children also need to learn to think about truths from Scripture as part of prac-ticing the discipline of meditation. Depending on their ages, you can either read Scriptures aloud to them or have them read verses you select for them on their own. Choose Scripture versions that are easy for children to understand such as *International Children's Bible* and *New Living Translation*.

> Children need to learn to think about truths from Scripture as part of practicing the discipline of meditation.

Since children need consistent label-ing of their sense of worth, belonging, and competence, begin with Scripture verses that give the truth about their worth. The goal is to guide children to think about what God tells them about their worth and His desire to have a relationship with them. You may say to children, "You mean so much to God that He sent Jesus to make it possible for you to live with Him forever. Listen to these words from God's book the Bible. 'Christ died for us' (Romans 5:6a, ICB). 'Jesus is alive' (Luke 24:23, NLT). 'God has said, 'I will never leave you; I will never forget you' (Hebrews 13:5b, ICB)."

Intentionally form their sense of belonging by having them think on verses about the truth of being a child of God and belonging to Him. "To all who received him [Jesus], to those who believed in his name, he gave the right to become children of God" (John 1:12). "You are all children of God through faith in Christ Jesus" (Galatians 3:26b, ICB).

Build their sense of competence by having them think about verses that teach the truth about competence. Competence results not just from successful experiences but dependence upon the Holy Spirit to teach, help, and guide. "God is working in you to help you want to do what pleases him. Then he gives you the power to do it" (Philippians 2:13, ICB).

As you guide children to think about God, refrain from talking during the experience. Instead, provide a way for children to draw or write in order to express what they think. Discussion may occur after the time of thinking is completed or later, in teachable moments.

Ideas For Children To Listen To The Ways And Words Of God

Intentional listening is an essential part of meditation. Listening experiences need to be modeled by those of us who guide children. The practice of listening also needs to be labeled for children. Labeling and modeling are the two most effective approaches for guiding children. Be creative about times and places to model, label, and encourage children in listening. Use both intentional strategies and unexpected teachable moments to help children experience listening and thinking about what they hear.

You may practice intentional listening while riding in the car with the windows open. Encourage children to listen for God's words and ways with thoughtful questions: "Listen, what does the rush and busyness of traffic sounds bring to your thoughts?" (A possible answer: people are in such a hurry, and they do not sing or play anymore.) Be sure to allow children time to give their thoughts and ideas.

A teachable moment may occur when you and your children hear the siren of an emergency vehicle. Ask the children what the sound is that they are hearing. Ask them what kinds of vehicles make the sound and why. Reinforce this teachable moment with a comment such as: "What do you think about when you hear that sound, and how might we pray?" (A possible answer: the sound may remind us to ask God to protect and give wisdom to those who are in trouble.)

Listening as you walk with children is another way to guide children to practice meditation. As you begin a walk, ask children to close their mouths but open their ears and eyes to look for and listen to creatures God has made. Say to them, "Look for colors and textures in trees, flowers, insects, animals, the sky, and clouds. Think on, or meditate on, what you see and hear. Remember and be ready to talk about what you see and hear when we return."

When a child seems distracted by something along the way such as a bee and begins to tell you the story about when she was stung by a bee, take the opportunity to use guided conversation to help the child and other children refocus. "Zaina, being stung by a bee is not very pleasant. Think about why God gave bees stingers. When we return from taking our walk and listening to all the different ways of God, you may share your thoughts about bee stings."

Teaching Tip:

Use guided conversation to help children refocus.

Ask questions to guide children's thinking towards God's nature of creating. "Why do you think God created rain?" "What does rain do for growing things?"

When a rainstorm begins, encourage children to listen to the rain, its speed, and the sound of the drops. An activity that allows both listening and participating is to invite children to make the sounds of a rainstorm.

Place your fingertips together and softly make the sound of the patter of beginning rain. Then place your hands on the upper part of your legs and make the sound of the rain increasing. Say, "The rain is coming down faster and harder." Begin softly clapping your hands, then clap louder and louder, faster and faster. Then without words, begin to slow down both the noise and the speed of the clapping. Move from clapping to tapping and then to silence. Ask questions to guide children's thinking towards God's nature of creating. "Why do you think God created rain?" "What does rain do for growing things?"

Choose to listen to the wind, the soft breezes, and the sounds of puffs and gusts. Listen also to the power of a strong wind. Listen to hail. Listen for the sounds the different sizes of the hail make as they hit the ground. Listen to snow. Hear the silence of the falling snowflakes. Ask, "What do the sounds you hear tell you about God?"

Listening to music is an easy way to practice meditation. Play music that your children know and enjoy. Instead of singing the music, ask them to stay still, not move or talk, just listen to the words. When finished, ask the children to describe what they were thinking as they listened to the words and music.

Recent statistics show some discouraging effects of technology upon our children. Eugene Peterson in his book, *The Jesus Way,* says, "A technologized world knows how to make things, knows how to get places, but is not conspicuous for living well."[2] This statement gives impetus for us to find ways to positively use today's technology. One way to use technology to help children practice listening is to create an iPod center. In the iPod center pictured here, children listen to Bible verses and practice thinking about God. As they listen, they write or draw their ideas about what the Bible verses tell them about God.

Use imagination to enhance listening times. Imagination, when directed toward God and His ways, can lead us into colorful and memorable times with Him. Give children the opportunity to use imagination while listening to a passage of Scripture. "Imagine that you are a friend of Noah's family and you are watching the family build a big boat. What would you say to them as you walk by their house?"

You may choose to help children learn the ancient tradition called *lectio divina,* which is a "guided" method to keep imagination focused on God's words and ways. Marti Watson, who has more than thirty years of experience as an educator and author, describes the use of *lectio divina* with children:

Because *lectio divina* is a slow and measured reading, choose an active story from the Bible, such as Daniel and the lion's den. Read the story aloud in a hushed and reverential way. Ask your children what stands out, providing adequate think-time. Children must be helped to approach the Bible this way; it doesn't come naturally to any of us. And remember, there are no right and wrong answers.

After all have had a chance to respond, read the story aloud again. This time ask what the setting looked like, what the lions sounded like, what the expression on Daniel's face was when he was thrown in the den, what the king and his court looked liked, and so on. Finally, read the story aloud one additional time, and then give everyone a chance to share what he or she heard as a personal message from the story. One person may hear the need for courage, while another may hear the need to trust God in the face of death.[3]

Ideas For Children To Hear And Understand God's Words And Ways

Children need guidance to hear and understand God's words and ways. As children hear God through His Word and His ways, it is not just for knowledge but also for understanding of the ways God speaks to us. The hearing part of the practice of meditation is not about how much is read or reading a portion quickly.

Guide children in multiple ways to use God's book the Bible for times of meditation. Create a time when you read aloud a meaningful, age-level appropriate portion, modeling how to read it when the purpose of reading is to listen, think about God, and hear His voice (meditation).

Read with thought to your tone of voice, inflection, and interest. Read slowly. Psalms and the gospels are a good place to start. You may also read out of a children's version such as the *International Children's Bible*. Ask the children to listen as you read and be ready to share their thoughts when you finish.

Build a positive attitude in children to want to hear and understand what God is saying about the best ways to be and do. One way is to have children listen to or read Psalm 119:33–34. "Teach me, O Lord, to follow your decrees; then I will keep them to the end. Give me understanding, and I will keep your law and obey it with all my heart." After reading this verse, ask, "What did you hear? What thoughts come to your mind when you to ask God to teach you His ways? What are two things you would like to understand about the way God is teaching you to live with Him and with others?"

Make Scripture memorization an intrinsic part of forming patterns of meditation. Select age-appropriate verses, and give children a variety.

Choose verses that give children thoughts of joy and happiness. "God is love" (1 John 4:8b). "Praise the Lord, for the Lord is good" (Psalm 135:3). "Lord, every morning you hear my voice. Every morning, I tell you what I need. And I wait for your answer" (Psalm 5:3, ICB). "Rejoice in the Lord always. I will say it again: Rejoice!" (Philippians 4:4).

Include verses to counteract peer pressures. "A friend loves at all times" (Proverbs 17:17). "Be kind and loving to each other. Forgive each other just as God forgave you in Christ" (Ephesians 4:32, ICB). "Let us think about each other and help each other to show love and do good deeds" (Hebrews 10:24, ICB).

> Make Scripture memorization an intrinsic part of forming patterns of meditation.

Children need to hear verses that give them the truth about their security to counteract the media and culture messages of fear and distrust. "I am with you always" (Matthew 28:20b). "I will never leave you" (Hebrews 13:5b, ICB). "So don't be afraid. The Lord your God is with you everywhere you go" (Joshua 1:9, ICB). "Do not be afraid; do not be discouraged" (Joshua 8:1).

I have discovered some effective skills to help children hear, understand, and use what God is speaking in ways that allow God to shape their thoughts, words, and actions. As you read through these skills and the examples of them with Psalm 119:33–34, please notice the concrete words used to explain the abstract ideas.

- ### Label

  To label means to give a child a familiar or concrete word for an unfamiliar word or abstract concept. After reading Psalm 119:33–34, label key words and phrases so children can understand them.

  Example: "'Teach me to follow your decrees' means 'Lord, teach me to be and do what you want me to be and do'."

  Parents and teachers who are aware that children need familiar and concrete words to build understanding label a great deal, naturally and easily, in a wide variety of experiences.

- ### Describe

  Children need to hear simple accounts of what God is saying. Use the skill of description to help children understand abstract spiritual and character ideas and images. As you guide children to understand Psalm 119:33–34, describe the word *decree*. Begin with words that are familiar to children.

  Example: "A decree is an order. One of God's decrees is to love God and love each other."

Another example is a way to describe the words *with-God life*. "We live our lives with God. He is with us all the time, in every place, helping us think and say the right things and be kind and forgiving to each other."

▪ **Explain**

To explain means to give a child reasons and definitions. Enhance the hearing of Psalm 119:33–34 with an explanation.

Example: "Asking God to teach us helps us to be able to be and do what He wants anytime, anyplace, anywhere, and throughout all of our lives."

▪ **Stimulate**

A child's understanding is built by stimulating curiosity. Use open-ended questions that call for a child to share attitudes, ideas, and opinions, not just memorized answers.

Example: "What did you like best about the ideas and direction in these words in Psalm 119:33–34 from God's book the Bible?"

Children need guidance to hear God's voice and sense His presence. Continue to help them label or name experiences and ideas they discover in their everyday, walk-around lives. This task is true for their spiritual experiences as well.

Sometimes adults take away a child's spiritual experience by not accepting what the child sees or hears. Sometimes adults take away a child's spiritual experience because they have not had a similar experience.

In the Old Testament, the young child Samuel and the elderly priest Eli have an experience that both illustrates an opportunity to hear God's voice and is an example of guiding a child to understand the hearing of God's voice.

> One night … the Lord called Samuel. Samuel answered, "I am here!" He ran to Eli and said, "I am here. You called me." But Eli said, "I didn't call you. Go back to bed." So Samuel went back to bed. The Lord called again, "Samuel!" Samuel again went to Eli and said, "I am here. You called me." Again Eli said, "I didn't call you. Go back to bed." Samuel did not yet know the Lord. The Lord had not spoken directly to him yet. The Lord called Samuel for the third time. Samuel got up and went to Eli. He said, "I am here. You called me." Then Eli realized the Lord was calling the boy. So he told Samuel, "Go to bed. If he calls you again, say,

'Speak, Lord. I am your servant, and I am listening.'" So Samuel went and lay down in bed. The Lord came and stood there. He called as he had before. He said, "Samuel, Samuel!" Samuel said, "Speak, Lord. I am your servant, and I am listening." (1 Samuel 3:2–10, ICB)

When my grandson Thomas was about four years old, he and his family traveled to my home in California for a week's visit. On Sunday we attended my church, where our service began with twenty minutes of worship. The congregation was standing, singing, and praising God when Thomas, who was also standing, raised his arms and slowly turned, moving his fingers, touching something we could not see. He said in a gentle, happy voice, "What is it, what is this, this soft wind?" We were able to label this experience for what it was, sensing the presence of God's Spirit!

Ways For You To Practice And Model Meditation

For the next seven days, using this passage of Scripture, try to think about God, listen, and hear His voice based on your enlarged understanding of meditation.

Finally, beloved, whatever is true, whatever is honorable, whatever is just, whatever is pure, whatever is pleasing, whatever is commendable, if there is any excellence and if there is anything worthy of praise, think about these things. Keep on doing the things that you have learned and received and heard and seen in me, and the God of peace will be with you. (Philippians 4:8–9, *The Renovaré Spiritual Formation Bible*, NRSV)

Reflect: What is your motivation to further explore the discipline of meditation (thinking about God, listening, and hearing God's voice)?

When and where in your everyday, walk-around life do you practice (or not) meditation?

Respond: Choose which of the following character virtues may help you enhance your practice of meditation. Circle one or more: compassion, forgiveness, integrity, respect, responsibility, initiative, cooperation, perseverance. (See the Appendix for definitions.)

God's compassion and love call to us. Pray for God's compassion and love toward you to drive your inner discipline and spiritual strength to meet each challenge or difficulty that keeps you from entering into the habit of thinking about God, listening, and hearing God's voice (meditation). You might begin by intentionally setting a time in your routine for meditation one or more days each week.

Think on Colossians 3:12–17.

Therefore, as God's chosen people, holy and dearly loved, clothe yourselves with compassion, kindness, humility, gentleness and patience. Bear with each other and forgive whatever grievances you may have against one another. Forgive as the Lord forgave you. And over all these virtues put on love, which binds them all together in perfect unity. Let the peace of Christ rule in your hearts, since as members of one body you were called to peace. And be thankful. Let the word of Christ dwell in you richly as you teach and admonish one another with all wisdom, and as you sing psalms, hymns and spiritual songs with gratitude in your hearts to God. And whatever you do, whether in word or deed, do it all in the name of the Lord Jesus, giving thanks to God the Father through him.

Activities And Guided Conversations For Children

Daily Practice

For younger children, be prepared to read one or more of the following verses: 1 John 4:8, "God is love"; Psalm 135:3, "Praise the LORD, for the LORD is good"; Matthew 28:20, "I am with you always"; Hebrews 13:5, ICB, "I will never leave you."

For older children, have a Bible for each child or a printout of these verses: "A friend loves at all times" (Proverbs 17:17); "Be kind and compassionate to one another, forgiving each other, just as in Christ God forgave you" (Ephesians 4:32); "So don't be afraid. The Lord your God is with you everywhere you go" (Joshua 1:9, ICB); "I will never leave you" (Hebrews 13:5, ICB); "Do not be afraid; do not be discouraged" (Joshua 8:1).

Guided Conversation

For younger children: "To practice thinking about God, listening, and hearing God's voice, I am going to read a short verse three times. The first two times you are to listen. The third time you may say the verse with me. Any questions? If you are ready, put your hand on your head. Okay, here we go. (Read the verse you chose.) What do you think God is saying to you in this verse?" (Allow children to respond. Then according to age-appropriate interest level and time, continue the same pattern with other short verses.)

For older children: "To practice thinking about God, listening, and hearing God's voice, I am giving you a 3 x 5 card (or a sticky note) for you to print a verse on. You may choose to place your card on your bathroom mirror or on the ceiling above your bed to enable you to read and think about what God is speaking to you. Here are the verses from which you may choose:

> "A friend loves at all times" (Proverbs 17:17); "Be kind and compassionate to one another, forgiving each other, just as in Christ God forgave you" (Ephesians 4:32); "So don't be afraid. The Lord your God is with you wherever you go" (Joshua 1:9, ICB); "I will never leave you" (Hebrews 13:5, ICB); "Do not be afraid; do not be discouraged" (Joshua 8:1).

"What else might you do to create a new daily practice to read Bible verses and take time to think about God, listen, and hear His voice? You might set a time that could be the same every day for five days in a row. What are some other ways to begin? (Allow responses.) What could be some other daily activities for the next five days?"

Three Times A Day

Think On Words From God's Book The Bible

Guided Conversation

"As followers of Jesus, three times during the day we may choose to think about words from God's book the Bible. Just before we fall asleep, we may have God's words be the last thing that we think about. When we wake up, we may have words from God's book the Bible be the first thing we think about to start the day. Also, we may choose to find a time during each day to read God's book the Bible to help us think about God's words and ways throughout our day.

"Let's start by creating a one-month calendar together. (A one-month blank calendar is provided at the end of this chapter.) What is needed to make your blank calendar into a calendar for this month? (Possible answers: name for the month, days of the week, numbers of the days.) Begin to add what is needed. You may also wish to use colors to decorate your calendar. This calendar is to help you be intentional about your times to read and think about Bible words. What day or days and what time of day would be best for you to read some Bible words? Color, draw, or write your choices on your calendar.

"To help you begin to read and think about God's words, I have printed the Bible verse Philippians 4:8 (ICB) on a card for each of you. This verse tells us what is good to think about. Let's read it together.

> Continue to think about the things that are good and worthy of praise. Think about the things that are true and honorable and right and pure and beautiful and respected.

"What would be a <u>true</u> thing we might think about? (Allow children's response. Possible answers: God loves me, I belong to God, I love God.) What would be an <u>honorable</u> idea we might think about? To honor means to give respect. What would be one way to give respect to others today? (Allow children's response. Possible answers: use respect words such as *please* and *thank you*, open a door for someone.) What would be a <u>right</u> thing we might think about?" (Continue this pattern throughout the verse, using the words *pure, beautiful,* and *respected*. Consider accomplishing this activity over several days.)

Think-Listen-Hear

For this activity you need a Bible for each child. You may wish to make a card for each child of the words of the song "Be Kind and Tenderhearted" provided at the end of this chapter. The words are from Ephesians 4:32. Words and music may be found in Sing Praise Song Book #87 G/L Publications. Or you may sing the words to the tune of a familiar song.

Guided Conversation

"Another way to think about, listen, and hear God's words and ways (meditation) is to sing Bible words. There is a song that has Bible words found in the Bible book named Ephesians. Here is a card with the words of the song called 'Be Kind and Tenderhearted.' Let's read the words together. Now let's sing them together.

"Now our task is to compare the words of the song to the Bible words. The Bible words are found in Ephesians chapter 4, verse 32. (Adapt the following to the appropriate age and experience the children you are serving have with the Bible.) Ephesians is found in the New Testament. Where is the New Testament found in the Bible? (Allow children to respond.) The first four books of the New Testament are Matthew, Mark, Luke, John. Please repeat them with me. Thank you. Now take your Bible and find the New Testament. Page through Matthew, Mark, Luke, and John. Then go past Acts, Romans, 1 Corinthians, 2 Corinthians, and Galatians. There it is—Ephesians. The big numbers are the chapters, so look for the big number 4. The small numbers are verses, so look for the small number 32. Let's read the verse out loud together.

"Now look again at the words of the song: 'Be kind and tender-hearted, forgiving one another, remembering the way that Jesus has forgiven you.' How are they alike or different from the words in Ephesians 4:32?"

What Is God Like?

Thoughts about what God is like are another part of meditation.

Guide children at the earliest ages to think about what God is like. What is God's nature and character? Begin to explore these three virtues of God: compassion, forgiveness, and integrity.

Guided Conversation

Compassion: "God is a compassionate God. Does God love the all the people of the world? (Allow children's response.) How do we know that God does love all the people of the world? (Allow children's response.) Draw some pictures or write some words to show some ways God tells you that He loves you."

Forgiveness: "God is the Great Forgiver. When we ask, He forgives us for all the wrong things we think and say and do. And God gives us Jesus and the Holy Spirit to help us choose what is right. What are some of the right things and the right ways God wants us to choose to be and to do? (Possible answers: be kind, especially to others who need friends. Use language that encourages others. Be ready to forgive.) Draw a picture or write some words about either a time you wished you knew you were forgiven or a time you were a forgiver."

Integrity: "God is a person of integrity; He always tells the truth. What are some true ideas He tells us? (Possible answers: I will never leave you; I am with you always.) Let's talk about other ideas or thoughts you have about God." (To encourage children to think 'out of the box,' you may ask a few of the following questions.

- What is His favorite color?

- What kind of sky did He make today?

- What do you think God is thinking right now?

But be sure, after each question you have asked, to give the child a turn to think of and ask a question.)

Choice And Conflict

Suggested items needed for this activity include lined paper for making lists and pencils or pens for each child, Bibles, and Bible verses printed on strips of paper. Place Bible verses in a basket or jar. (See reinforcement page at the end of chapter for verses.)

Note: For younger children, you may wish to have them make a picture list by cutting out magazine pictures and pasting them on the lined paper. Simple ideas include brushing teeth, combing hair, and deciding what to wear.

Guided Conversation

"Most days we have times when we need or want to make a choice. And on some days we are in conflict with some person or some activity. It is helpful to think about, listen, and hear the truth of God's words and ways (meditation) in order to make the best or most constructive choices, especially in times of disagreement or conflict.

"Let's begin by thinking of and making a list of the kinds of choices you make each day. (Allow children time to think.) Now turn your paper over and list the kinds of conflicts you have had this week. Maybe you were invited to two birthday parties that happen on the same day at the same time. Or you and your best friend had an argument. You may wish to add some "What would I do if …" questions to your list.

"In this container I have several Bible verses. You may take turns drawing out a slip of paper and reading the verse aloud so that we may listen and then think how the verse might help us with one of the choices or one of the conflicts we have on the two lists we made."

Name_____Date _____

My Calendar

Sunday	Monday	Tuesday	Wednesday	Thursday	Friday	Saturday

"Be Kind And Tenderhearted"

Be kind and tenderhearted, forgiving one another, remembering the way that Jesus has forgiven you.

Be kind and tenderhearted, forgiving one another, remembering the way that Jesus has forgiven you.

Bible Verses

Cut the following Bible verses apart into strips of paper, fold, and place in a container from which children may draw the verses.

"Do not make plans to hurt your neighbors. And don't make false promises."

Zechariah 8:17, ICB

"Be kind and compassionate to one another, forgiving each other, just as in Christ God forgave you."

Ephesians 4:32, NIV

"Do not be angry with each other, but forgive each other. If someone does wrong to you, then forgive him. Forgive each other because the Lord forgave you."

Colossians 3:13, ICB

"Love each other like brothers and sisters. Give your brothers and sisters more honor than you want for yourselves."

Romans 12:10, ICB

"Live in harmony with one another. Do not be proud, but be willing to associate with people of low position. Do not be conceited."

Romans 12:16, NIV

"Do not lie to each other."

Colossians 3:9b, NIV

"Everyone should be quick to listen, slow to speak and slow to become angry."

James 1:19, NIV

Chapter Two

The Practice of Prayer—Talk with God

We do not know how to pray as we should. But the Spirit himself speaks to God for us, even begs God for us. The Spirit speaks to God with deep feelings that words cannot explain.

Romans 8:26, ICB

Be joyful always; pray continually; give thanks in all circumstances, for this is God's will for you in Christ Jesus.

1 Thessalonians 5:16–18

"Dear God, I bet it is very hard for you to love all of everybody in the whole world. There are only four people in our family, and I can never do it."

Nan

Prayer is how we talk with God and share in a growing love relationship with Him. Prayer may take place as a private, personal experience with God. It may also be a community experience with God and family, friends, or larger groups of followers of Jesus. My child friendly wording for *prayer* is "talking with God, listening to God, and spending time with God."

Prayer is talking with God, listening to God, and spending time with God.

The Practice Of Prayer For Followers Of Jesus

As you enter into the practice of prayer, it may be as natural as breathing. Or you may find that you struggle with a time, or place, or pattern of how to talk with God. Richard Foster offers some encouragement: "We will never have pure enough motives, or be good enough, or know enough in order to pray rightly. We simply must set all these things aside and begin praying. In fact, it is in the very act of prayer itself—the intimate, ongoing interaction with God—that these matters are cared for in due time."[1]

The simple truth is that there is no one way to pray. What is important is to practice talking with God anytime, anyplace, anywhere, and about anything.

The practice of prayer may be encouraged in you and in your children with the suggestions and examples that follow.

Model Ways To Pray

Teacher and parent examples of prayer are more powerful than anything you say to children about prayer. That said, do not panic as you take on this adventure. It is possible to become a model of prayer as a natural part of your everyday, walk-around life.

Teacher and parent examples of prayer are more powerful than anything you say to children about prayer.

Jesus modeled prayer as an integral part of His everyday experiences. Sometimes Jesus' prayers were formal, head bowed, eyes closed. Sometimes He prayed as He walked and talked with the people and His disciples. Many times He prayed with individuals, sometimes with small groups, and sometimes with very large groups of people. Often He prayed alone. Jesus gives us this model that we may choose to adopt, practice, and make a treasured and lifelong pattern of His many ways of prayer.

Be intentional to pray about everything you encounter in your everyday experiences until it becomes a well-established pattern in your life that children regularly observe. "I can't remember where I put the keys to the car. Please, Lord, help me remember."

Pray for others, those you know and those you see in your daily interactions. Listen to conversations and interactions for guidance about ways to pray for the people God has around you. "The lady in front of me is so upset with the clerk. Please help them communicate with each other."

Pray for guidance to know and understand God's direction for your life. "Lord Jesus, please tell us where you would have us live and what the best school is for our children." "Lord, help me to see and respond to what you have for me to be and do today."

Be spontaneous and concrete with your prayers. Pets and parking places are concrete, everyday stuff about which to pray. It doesn't matter what your belief is about where puppies go when they die. Children love their pets and want to ask Jesus to take care of them. So thank Jesus for pets, ask Him for protection and health of children's pets, and accept their ideas of where a pet goes when it dies.

After I broke my left arm, six months later had rotator surgery on the right arm, and a year later broke my left leg, my grandchildren heard me ask God for close parking places due to the injuries. That prayer evolved over time. Now that I am recovered from those injuries, my prayer for parking places has changed. I now say, "Please help us find a parking place that is best for our health, and give those who aren't so healthy the close places."

Develop patterns of prayer that are age appropriate. In your home, make it possible for your children to hear and see you pray in everyday times. Pray with them in the morning. Pray at mealtimes using different prayers and prayer songs. Pray with your children at bedtime.

In a classroom or church program setting, consider beginning the time with prayer. If you teach in public school, it may not be a choice to do so out loud, but you may regularly invite the children to a moment of silence as you pray silently for the needs in your classroom.

Pray with children before their sporting or club events. Pray specifically for coaches to be good leaders, referees to make correct calls, judges to have the ability to make just decisions, and children to be honest and choose attitudes that are respectful and responsible.

In a preschool setting, pray at snack time using simple, concrete words. "Thank you, God, for this food." Encourage children to teach each other the prayers they pray in their home at mealtimes. Ending time is often a time to model prayers of thanks and prayers of compassion for needs that have surfaced during class such as Susie's scraped knee and Johnny's cough.

Compassion
Forgiveness
Integrity
Respect
Responsibility
Initiative
Cooperation
Perseverance

Focus On God's Character

Intentional, godly character formation takes place in tandem with each spiritual practice as God's character virtues are labeled and modeled. So when you pray aloud with children, label and describe God's character. This prayer, as an example, labels and describes the virtues of forgiveness and compassion: "Dear forgiving God, thank you for talking with us. Thank you for your compassion, love, and care for us. Thank you for forgiving us when we tell you we have thought, said, or done wrong things. Help us to choose to forgive ourselves and others. Thank you for always loving and forgiving us. In Jesus' name we pray, amen."

The goal of intentionally focusing on God's character through the practice of prayer is to guide children to know and experience God's character in ways that result in a desire to be like Him. Think of ways your prayers may reflect God's character. Integrity, for example, is another of God's virtues. You may say in a prayer with children, "Wow, Jesus, thank you for the way you tell the truth. Help us be people who tell the truth and reflect your integrity to our family and friends."

The model of regular, intentional, lifelong patterns of prayer provides opportunities for God's character virtue of perseverance to be formed in you as well as in your children. Perseverance is continual, steady effort made to fulfill some purpose, goal, task, or commitment. It means persistence in spite of difficulties, opposition, or discouragement. Perseverance is the refusal to give up when things are difficult. It is a habit to follow through and finish what was started.

Set aside time for prayer each day. Choose a place where you can pray without interruption. In addition, be intentional to communicate regularly with God at other times and places throughout your day. Label these patterns for children, and encourage them to make similar choices.

Persevere (never, never give up) to regularly communicate with God in spite of your circumstances. The practice of prayer deepens your connection to God. The lifelong pattern of prayer results in an intimate, loving, trusting, and secure place where your mind and will finds His counsel and guidance.

> Persevere (never, never give up) to regularly communicate with God in spite of your circumstances.

Ideas To Guide Children In The Practice Of Prayer

In addition to modeling prayer for children, guide them into the practice of prayer in their lives using these basic principles.

- **Make Prayer Simple and Short**

    Many adult prayers convince children that prayer is difficult and boring. Make yours simple. At meals and snack time, use a short prayer such as, "For health and strength and daily food we praise your name, O Lord." For bedtime and ending times, say, "Thank you for your loving care round about us everywhere." Then you and your children may each pray spontaneous thank-you or blessing prayers.

Ask children what they would like to pray about, and then use the words they give you in your prayer. "Lord, we pray for Alisha's grandmother, that you will help her with the pain in her stomach."

■ **Create Prayer Experiences**

Remind children that God wants us to talk with Him about everything: family; needs; friends; school; food; and wrong thoughts, words, or actions. We can talk with God about everything! A prayer list is a way to create a physical experience to help prayer become concrete. A prayer list also encourages children who respond to a daily chore chart and are highly visual. The list needs to be simple and easy for children to use. A prayer list sample is included as a reinforcement page at the end of this chapter.

■ **Give Children Explanations About Ways to Pray**

It is helpful for children to establish some concrete ways to talk with and listen to God. Remember to explain to children with reasons and definitions. "You may pray silently inside, where only God hears." "You may pray out loud." "You may talk with God anytime, anyplace, and anywhere."

■ **Label and Describe Ways God Answers Prayer**

Guide children to understand ways God answers prayer. Read and discuss Scripture verses that talk about how God hears people's prayers and responds to them. "Jeremiah 33:3 says, 'Call to me and I will answer you and tell you great and unsearchable things you do not know.' When we hear or read the words *call to me* in this verse, God is asking us to talk with Him."

Another way to concretely label and describe ways God answers prayer is to connect a firsthand, everyday experience to four truths of how God answers prayer. Use a picture of a traffic light and a star. Sometimes God says yes (green). Sometimes God says no (red). Sometimes God says to slow down (yellow). And sometimes God says, "I have something better" (star).

If traffic lights are not a part of your culture, use circles for the children to color green, red, and yellow. Descriptions become clear and simple with this reading and coloring activity. An activity for this idea and a reinforcement page is at the end of this chapter.

- **Use Music to Describe Talking with God**
  Music is an easy and effective way for children to understand more about ways to talk with God. I have included a reinforcement page at the end of this chapter that contains the words from two songs that label and describe prayer for children. (These songs are available on the "It Takes Love"[2] CD.)

- **Guide Children to Listen When Talking with God**
  An important part of prayer is listening to God. It is similar to listening during meditation but different because prayer listening is a two-way communication. When we pray, we are talking with God *and* listening to His response.

Teaching Tip:

Children's intellectual development and spiritual development require physical experiences, actions, and movement.

Following is an interaction I use to guide children to listen to God in prayer. It incorporates physical experiences, actions, and movement to help children think and learn. I have used it with children as young as four and as old as ten.

"Prayer is talking with God. But sometimes it is right and good to listen quietly to God. Prayer is also listening to God. Here is a fun way to prepare to listen.

"First, we will make noise and then make quiet so we are ready to hear what God has to say to us. Please stand and make noise by clapping your hands as loud as you can and stomping your feet until I say stop. Ready? Go! Make noise. (Allow children to make noise for 30 to 45 seconds.)

"Stop. Now make quiet. Begin by sitting down. No sounds at all until I say stop. Ready? Go! Make quiet. (Allow children to make quiet for 30 to 45 seconds. Repeat this pattern again, increasing the 'make quiet' time to 60 to 75 seconds.)

"As we continue to make quiet, listen for what God is saying to you. (Pause and allow time for listening.) If you would like to share with all of us what God is saying to you, please do so now." (Pause and allow responses from children. Do not force any reply. Trust the Holy Spirit to speak to and through the children. The Holy Spirit speaks that which agrees with the whole of Scripture.)

▪ **Pray Blessing Prayers**

Words can be affirming or destructive; touch can be healthy or demeaning and impure. The realization that many children are marred by accidental, unintentional, and sometimes intentionally hurtful words or touch of parents or other people motivates us to learn to bless the children we serve.

Blessing is a biblical expression that means to extend a hand or bring a touch upon a person. With the enrichment of touch, words spoken in blessings are creative and powerful. Both Old Testament practices of biblical blessing and New Testament examples of parents bringing their children to Jesus for blessings set the pattern for us to bestow blessings on children at home and in community. And we may make it an intentional strategy to encourage children to bless siblings, other family members, and friends.

Children are a gift and heritage from the Lord. Psalm 127:3 says, "Sons are a heritage from the LORD, children a reward from him." An inheritance may be given that is material wealth, but children hold before us an opportunity to experience wealth that is not material. They give an opportunity for us to rejoice in children who are inconvenient, behavior challenges,

> Children hold before us an opportunity to experience wealth that is not material.

not related to us, or we would have no occasion to address except that they were plopped into our life.

As followers of Jesus, we are called to convey redemption and grace to children and do what we can to recover whatever damage may have been done to them. The combination of words and touch leaves children with the deep sense of being loved, accepted, cared for, and valued. Blessings speak hope, life, and a sense of belonging, worth, and competence into them. Blessings lay the groundwork for children's inheritance to multiply with each generation.

One special time of blessing children occurred at the end of the kindergarten year at a school where I was serving. We invited parents to prepare blessings for their children, giving them guidance to share the positive attributes and attitudes they had experienced with their children. On the day of the event, the children sat in a semi-circle on the floor with parents sitting behind their children. Each child was invited one at a time to come forward and kneel. Then the child's parents were invited to come behind and lay hands on the child's head or shoulders and say the blessings they had prepared.

The blessings given that day were specific about each child. They sounded something like this one: "Caleb, your name means faith, devotion. We see your tender attitude toward your friends and ours. You are able to see the needs of others and often ask us to pray with you for them. We ask God to continue to bless us and to bless you as you grow, learn, love God, and obey His ways. We love you and thank God for sending you to us."

Be encouraged to lay hands on your children and bless them on special occasions such as birthdays, family gatherings, and holidays.

- **Pray Prayers of Protection**
  Intentional prayers of protection surround us and our family and friends with comforting words and peace-giving conversation with God. "Protect us with the life of Christ." "Protect us as we travel." "Guard our minds and thoughts from destructive attitudes and actions." "The Lord will protect you from harm; He will protect your life. The Lord will protect your coming and going both now and forever."

- **Use Flash Prayer**
  Frank Laubach in his many books on prayer encourages us to learn ways to live so that "to see anybody will be to pray! To hear anybody, as these children talking, that boy crying, may be to pray!"[3]

Try talking with God aloud when you and your children are in a conflict situation. Label the opportunity to pray a "flash prayer." "Lord God, please bring your peace, settlement, and acceptance to these people who are in conflict and disagreement."

As you interact with children about talking with God, encourage them to make it a pattern to "flash" prayers straight toward people, asking for the love of the Lord and an awareness of His presence to become a part of their lives. When you travel to an airport or are in a plane, stand in line at the grocery store, or wait for a parent to finish a conversation, invite Jesus to be there, waiting with you. Ask Jesus to talk with the people around you, to tell them how much He loves them and forgives them and wants to give them good things and a life with Him.

Ways For You To Practice And Model Prayer

Reflect: Beliefs drive behavior and attitudes drive actions. What beliefs or attitudes drive you to further explore the practice of talking with God, listening to God, and spending time with God?

Where in your everyday, walk-around life do you talk with God, Jesus, and the Holy Spirit?

Respond: Nothing is more influential or more detrimental in the formation of spiritual life in children than the power of quiet example. Choose one of the suggested prayer ideas presented in this chapter to practice for the next week. Make a note of your choice.

Character drives conduct. What character virtue(s), intentionally applied, will help you accomplish the practice of prayer? Circle one or more: compassion, forgiveness, integrity, respect, responsibility, initiative, cooperation, perseverance.

Pray continually for God's character to drive your prayer conduct and give you spiritual strength to meet each challenge or difficulty that keeps you from entering into lifelong patterns of prayer.

Activities And Guided Conversations For Children

Four Ways

Provide a picture of a traffic light or, if traffic lights are not a part of your culture, create circles for the children to color green, red, and yellow, and provide the words from the reinforcement page. Or make a copy for each child of the reinforcement page "Four Ways God Answers You." Provide crayons or colored markers.

Guided Conversation

"This reading and coloring activity is a way to think and talk about ways God answers prayers. Here is a page for you to read words with me. As we read, you may make choices about coloring the circles and star.

"Sometimes God says, 'Yes!' What traffic light color would you choose to say 'yes'? (Allow child(ren's) response and then affirm.) Color the circle green.

"Sometimes God says, 'No.' What traffic light color would you choose to say 'no'? (Allow child(ren's) response and then affirm.) Color the circle red. Trust God to tell you 'no' when you ask for something that is not best for you.

"Sometimes God says, 'Slow down; wait awhile.' What traffic light color would you choose to say 'slow down; wait a while'? (Allow child(ren's) response and then affirm.) Color the circle yellow. God is wise, and He will answer at the right time and in the best way.

"Sometimes God says, 'I have something better.' Color the star with your favorite color. Trust God to make the right choice for you."

My Prayer List

Make a copy for each child of the reinforcement page "My Prayer List." Provide pencils or pens, crayons or colored markers.

Guided Conversation

"What do you talk about when you talk with your mom or dad, a sister or a brother, or your friends? (Allow children to respond. Possible answers: family; friends;

school; food; wrong thoughts, words, or actions.) God wants us to talk with Him about everything. Even about stuff you think you cannot talk about with anyone else.

"We may know that God desires to talk with us because of these words from His Bible book. 'Do not worry about anything. But pray and ask God for everything you need. And when you pray, always give thanks' (Philippians 4:6, ICB).

"Here is a simple prayer list to help you with three 'talk with God' ideas. The first idea is to think what you would like to talk about with God. The second idea is to keep track of when you started to talk with God about this specific idea. The third is to keep track of what God said.

"Begin by printing in the prayer list what you would like to talk about with God. Then you may put today's date. What would you print in the third column?" (Allow child(ren) to respond.)

Other Ways To Practice Prayer

"Always pray for all God's people."
Ephesians 6:18b, ICB

Read the reinforcement page "Other Ways to Practice Prayer" found at the end of the chapter to become familiar with the activity, and then make a copy of it for each child.

Guided Conversation

"Think about the different ways there are to talk with God. What are some of the ideas on your paper?" (Allow children's response to each of the ideas, and guide them to write words or draw pictures of the different ways to talk with God.)

Listen

Prayer is talking with God, listening to God, and spending time with God.

Prepare a place of quiet and comfort for you and the child(ren) you are serving.

Guided Conversation

"Often we think of prayer as just talking with God. But being with family and friends we love includes talking *and* listening. The same is true with God. God listens to us, and we listen to Him. One way to think about prayer is being together with God, just hanging out together, talking and listening.

"Let's spend some time praying together. Find a comfortable position. Make your body still and silent. Breathe slowly and softly. In the quietness of your mind and body, think with God. Be aware of God's presence with you in every part of you: the part that thinks—your mind; the part you see—your body; and that part inside you—your spirit.

"Picture all the people who love you. Look with God at these people you love. Is there anything special you want to tell God about anyone? Is someone having a birthday? Is someone sick? Is someone doing something special? Is any one of the people you love lonely? Silently talk with God about whatever it might be. (Pause.)

"Now you and God look at the people you love and those who love you, and love them together. (Wait a minute or two.)

"Now silently enjoy God's presence and His loving you. (Wait a minute or two.)

"Remember, you can listen like this anytime, anyplace. All you need is yourself and your willingness to be quiet and enjoy God loving you. No one is able to give God your love but you. And no one is able to receive God's love for you except you. It is important for you and God to enjoy each other's company when you pray.

Popcorn Prayer

For popcorn prayer, you and your child(ren) need an attitude of joy and fun. Guide child(ren) to sit in a comfortable place and position. For a group of children, a circle creates an informal community.

Guided Conversation

"Popcorn prayer is a fun way to talk with God. First begin to think about what you would like to say to God. You may use just one or two words or a whole sentence or two. When you are ready, jump up and talk with God out loud. Then sit. Something that is said by another person may remind you of something you would like to talk with God about. So you may jump up and talk about that idea too. Just like popcorn popping, we may continue to pop up and talk about all of the things we want to say out loud to God."

Four Ways God Answers You

Sometimes God says, "Yes!" Color the circle green.

Sometimes God says, "No!" Color the circle red.
Trust God to tell you "no" when you ask for something
that is not best for you.

Sometimes God says, "Slow down; wait awhile."
Color the circle yellow. God is wise and will answer
at the right time and the best way.

Sometimes God says, "I have something better."
Color the star with your favorite color. Trust God
to make the right choice for you.

I ASKED GOD

Lyrics and Music by Douglas C. Eltzroth *

I asked God for something special
And He said, "Yes, that's a green light. Go!"
I asked God for something special.
He said, "Yes," not "no."

CHORUS:
Because He loves me and knows
What is very best for me. (Repeat)

I asked God for something special
And He said, "No, that's a red light.
Stop."
I asked God for something special.
He said, "Absolutely not!"
(CHORUS)
I asked God for something special
And He said, "Wait, that's a yellow light. Slow."
I asked God for something special
And He will let me know.
(CHORUS)
Sometimes He gives answers,
Not red or yellow or green.
Much better than I asked for,
Much better than my dreams.
It was not on my prayer list.
He thought it up for me.
Much better than I hoped for,
Exactly what I need!

(CHORUS)

I CAN TALK WITH GOD

Lyrics and Music by Douglas C. Eltzroth *

I can talk with God anytime
I can talk with God anywhere
We can talk about anything
And He hears my prayer
He's always there
Anytime, I can talk with God anywhere
We can talk about anything
And He hears my prayer
He's always there
He always hears my prayer
I can talk with God with my seatbelt on
I can talk with God when my Mom is gone
I can talk with God when my friend
can't play
It doesn't matter what time of day
I can talk with God if I'm bowing my head
I can talk with God if I'm laying in bed
I can talk with God just running around
It doesn't matter if I'm up or down
And the list goes on and on and on
and on and on
(Refrain)

I can talk with God when I'm climbing a tree
I can talk with God down on my knees
I can talk with God right before a meal
It doesn't matter about the way I feel
I can talk with God if I'm feeling sad
I can talk with God when I'm really mad
I can talk with God when I'm afraid of the night
It doesn't matter if it's dark or light
And the list goes on and on and on
and on and on
(Refrain)

I can talk with God when I'm singing a song
I can talk with God just walking along
I can talk with God about the problems I've had
It doesn't matter if it's good or bad
I can talk with God about surprise things
I can talk with God about everything
I can talk with God, Oh yes I can and
It doesn't matter if it's anyplace, anybody,
Anyhow, anymore, anyone, anything
Anyway, anytime, any old "any" at all
(Refrain) * Used by permission.

My Prayer List

"Do not worry about anything. But pray and ask God for everything you need. And when you pray, always give thanks." Philippians 4:6, ICB

What I Am Praying About	Date I Began To Pray	On This Date God Said…
_____	_____	_____
_____	_____	_____
_____	_____	_____
_____	_____	_____
_____	_____	_____
_____	_____	_____

Other Ways To Practice Prayer

"Always pray for all God's people."
Ephesians 6:18b, ICB

One way to pray is "thank-you" words.
Add some of your thank-you words to the words in the circle.

Another way to pray is to ask for help for ourselves and ask for help for other people. "Please, God, help my dad recover from the flu." "Please, God, help me be a compassionate person."

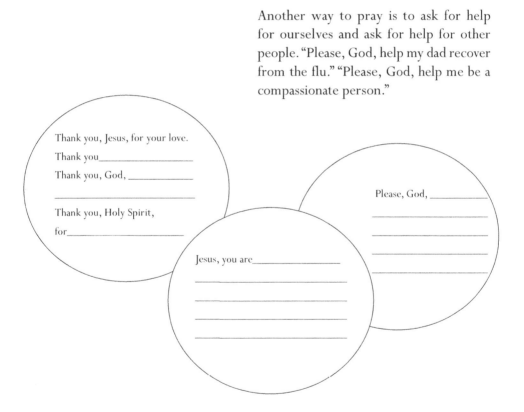

Thank you, Jesus, for your love.
Thank you_____
Thank you, God, _____
_____
Thank you, Holy Spirit,
for_____

Jesus, you are_____
_____
_____
_____
_____

Please, God, _____
_____
_____
_____
_____

Talk with Jesus about the fun things you are enjoying. Give praise to Him for who He is.

Chapter Three

The Practice of Study—Read, Observe, and Be Informed by God's Words and Ways

Do not be conformed to this world, but be transformed by the renewing of your minds, so that you may discern what is the will of God—what is good and acceptable and perfect.

Romans 12:2, NRSV

Do not change yourselves to be like the people of this world. But be changed within by a new way of thinking. Then you will be able to decide what God wants for you. And you will be able to know what is good and pleasing to God and what is perfect.

Romans 12:2, ICB

Thomas asked, "How did Jesus create the world before Jesus was born?"

The aim of the practice of spiritual disciplines is to replace destructive patterns of thought, belief, attitude, and conduct with constructive patterns of thought, belief, attitude, and conduct. Or in other words, to create life-giving practices that become lifelong patterns and habits that reflect God's character and the ways of Jesus. Spiritual disciplines enable us to know God more fully and experience Him more continuously in our everyday lives.

The practice of study brings us to a "new way of thinking" (Romans 12:2, ICB) about life and living and life with God. The practice of study forms the habit of searching for God's words and ways to answer life's important questions.

The Practice Of Study For Followers Of Jesus

We practice this discipline of study by reading the Bible. We practice this discipline of study by observation. And we practice this discipline of study by gathering information, or being informed. My child friendly wording for *study* is "read the Bible, observe, and be informed by God's words and ways."

> The practice of *study* is read the Bible, observe, and be informed by God's words and ways.

The intentional reading of God's book the Bible renews our minds so that we have the thoughts, beliefs, and attitudes of Christ. A Christ-like mind enables us to observe and interact with people, events, choices, conflicts, and situations as God views them.

The spiritual discipline of study includes gaining knowledge about the natural world through observation. Observation informs our conclusions about who we are and how we fit into God's master plan of creation. The orderliness of the natural world testifies to God's authority and power. The sun gives us light each day, and the moon follows its twenty-eight day cycle.

The natural world also testifies to God's nature and character of compassion, forgiveness, and integrity. This spring I observed two robins building their nest. Daily the mom and dad robins cared for each other by taking turns on the nest. One day it rained, and I noticed both of them compassionately cuddled together, protecting each other and their eggs. Such an example of God's compassion in nature!

Think with me about how you are informed about God's words and ways. How do you know what you know about God? Not just what you know with your mind, like memorized Scripture or Bible stories, but about Him personally as He relates to you. How do you pass on to children what you know about God that is deep in your spirit? What makes your life with God exciting and full of energy and joy? What is it about God that, in the midst of the maintenance of life and the hard, desert times of life, carries you?

The discipline of study includes being informed about who God says we are. Keep in mind, first, that *our beliefs drive our behavior*. We behave based on what we believe. When people believe God loves them all the time, their choice of obedience is driven by compassion, love, and kindness toward themselves and others. When people believe they have worth in God's eyes only when they are obedient and demonstrate behaviors that are good, they behave as though they must earn His love.

Second, keep in mind that *our attitudes drive our actions*. The positive attitudes we choose cause us to act in positive ways; the negative attitudes we choose result in actions that are negative. When people choose an attitude of love and service to others, their actions reflect enjoyment and fulfillment. When people choose an attitude of duty over loving and caring for others, their actions become full of jealousy and resentment.

Teaching Tip:

Beliefs drive behavior.

Attitudes drive actions.

Character drives conduct.

Third, keep in mind that *our character drives our conduct*. Our character is a collection of virtues and vices formed in us. How we conduct our lives demonstrates our wealth or poverty of character. When people's conduct includes forgiveness, they cease blaming others. When their conduct lacks forgiveness, they become revengeful.

Many followers of Jesus live out a life of "mistaken identity" rather than one that accurately portrays who God says they are. They believe they are flawed, so they behave as if they are flawed. Their actions are driven by their attitude of trying to live out who they think they should become. They try hard and struggle to improve themselves, but their poverty of character betrays them. They are attempting to conduct their lives to create an identity they mistakenly think God expects.

Many followers of Jesus trust a mistaken belief that they have failed God, which triggers a belief that He is disappointed with them and even blames them. This belief drives the behavior of "mask wearing" in the community. Others are not able to live with the thoughts of their perceived failure, so they delude themselves into believing that by their own achievements, they have an amazing spiritual life. Both of these mistaken beliefs gradually lead to a mistaken identity.

An intentional strategy to discover who God says you are is to ask a close friend to write a list of positive things he or she sees in you that reflect your nature and character. Things on the list might include compassionate, ability to be forgiving, grateful attitudes, creative, wisdom, reliable, respectful, truth teller, and sense of humor.

Why do some followers of Jesus find it so hard to have someone tell them the positive virtues they see in them? It is healthy and life giving to hear from another how God is forming His nature and character in you.

Another intentional strategy to discover your identity is to search the Scripture for verses regarding your identity in Christ. We belong to God (Eph. 1:5). We are the children of God (John 1:12). We are chosen by God (Col 3:12). We are Christ's friend (John 15:15).

Model Study In Your Communities

The model is more powerful than spoken words. What you are and do is more powerful than what you say. One other way of saying this truth is, "Actions speak louder than words." In *The Kingdom Life,* a collection of writings on discipleship and spiritual formation, Bill Thral and Bruce McNicol speak of a simple law of communication. In their words, the Law of Communication states, "Environments are more powerful than words, no matter how carefully those words are crafted."[1]

It is my belief that a large factor in the formation of the spiritual life of children is the nature of the children's communities, which is determined by the spiritual and character life of the key influencers in the children's life. The family is a child's primary community. Other communities that influence a child are schools, community resource centers, organized sports clubs, churches, synagogues, Sunday school, confirmation classes, communicant classes, catechism classes, and synagogue classes.

As children participate in these communities, they "study" the beliefs that drive the behavior, the attitudes that drive the actions, and the character that drives the conduct of the community members. Children imitate what they observe about beliefs, attitudes, and actions. As those of us who are followers of Christ become aware of the power of modeling in our community, we must strive intentionally to be models that live out the covenant relationship we are instructed by God to keep and to pass on to our children.

> Love GOD, your God, with your whole heart: love him with all that's in you, love him with all you've got! Write these commandments that I've given you today on your hearts. Get them inside of you and then get them inside your children. Talk about them wherever you are, sitting at home or walking in the street; talk about them from the time you get up in the morning to when you fall into bed at night. Tie them on your hands and foreheads as a reminder; inscribe them on the doorposts of your homes and on your city gates (Deuteronomy 6: 5–9, MSG).

I have recently become aware of the importance for followers of Jesus to model a correct and healing understanding of grace. When a correct and healing understanding of grace becomes a part of a community, people accept faults, flaws, poor choices, and mistakes; and they give support to those who must live out the consequences. As we live out grace towards our children and others, our communities become places where God, the "God of all grace," lives (1 Peter 5:10; 1 Corinthians 15:10).

Bill Thral and Bruce McNicol, in their chapter "Communities of Grace," describe the effect of God's grace on our lives.

> Grace is much more than a theological position. Grace extends a long way beyond the means of our salvation; grace is the very basis for our maturing and our life together. Grace is a real, a present-tense reality that weaves around and through every moment of even our worst day. God's gift of grace continuously and always surrounds us.[2]

First and foremost, the forming of communities of grace starts with trusting God and trusting others. If communities are filled with judgmental and critical attitudes and people who break trust and lack commitment, then it is likely the children's attitudes, trust, and commitment become what their communities are modeling.

Teaching Tip:

Make it a habit to consistently model, label, and describe beliefs and attitudes of grace.

Our task, as people who are followers of Jesus, is to create communities of grace where we model trust, commitment, belonging, and security in concrete ways that allow children to see, touch, taste, hear, and smell their communities as places where God lives. Keep in mind that more is caught than taught. Make it a habit to consistently *model, label,* and *describe* beliefs and attitudes of grace:

- The truth that Jesus loves us just as we are and never leaves us
- The truth that the things we think and say and do that are wrong do not keep Jesus from us
- The truth that Jesus, who is grace, actually puts His arm around us when we have thought, said, or done wrong
- The truth that God helps us look at our wrong from His view

Take advantage of teachable moments to demonstrate grace. For example, most children test out the telling of a lie. To demonstrate grace, choose an incident in which a child knows what the consequence of breaking a rule and telling a lie would be and yet chooses to do what is wrong.

A conversation of grace might sound like this: "Fiona, you lied about taking cookies without asking permission. The consequence is that you give up dessert for the next three times we have dessert." Fiona might respond, "I know I lied, and I apologize. I get it! No dessert for the next three times." You reply, "But this time, Fiona, I am going to grant you grace, which means that even though your lie earned not having dessert for the next three dessert times, you may have dessert tonight. I *choose* to trust you to make the right choice in the future to ask for permission to take cookies."

With-God communities of grace are the most effective environments to provide examples and demonstrate to children that God is with His people, that He always desires to love and care for us, and that in return we are to love Him.

Focus On God's Character

The regular, intentional study of God's character gives us the understanding of who God desires us to become. God's book the Bible tells us about His nature and character. The three character virtues of God that I begin to study with children are compassion, forgiveness, and integrity.

Compassion
Forgiveness
Integrity
Respect
Responsibility
Initiative
Cooperation
Perseverance

God is a compassionate God. 1 John 4:16 says, "God is love." Compassion is sympathy for someone else's suffering or misfortune, together with the desire to help, and appropriate action for his or her benefit. That definition may be made simple for younger children: Compassion is a desire to help and care for others. We have the choice of being compassionate or indifferent. We may choose to be kind, have sympathy for others' suffering, and desire to help others, which is compassion. Or we may choose to be uninterested in others and without concern for their suffering, which is indifference.

God is a forgiver. To forgive means to no longer blame or be angry with someone who has hurt or wronged you, including yourself. To forgive means to pardon or excuse a wrong thought, word, attitude, or action without condition. We have the choice of being forgivers or people of revenge. Colossians 3:13 says, "Bear with each other and forgive whatever grievances you may have against one another. Forgive as the Lord forgave you." When people practice forgiveness in their community, they break the cycle of revenge. When a person experiences forgiveness, he or she is freed from guilt and feelings of failure.

God is a person of integrity. Integrity is the strength and firmness of character that results in consistent sincerity and honesty. People of integrity keep their word. We have the choice of being people of integrity or people who are dishonest. Titus

2:7b says, "In your teaching show integrity." When people practice integrity, they keep their promises, tell the truth, and make and keep commitments.

The practice of the spiritual discipline of study forms beliefs that drive behavior. Dallas Willard describes belief as "when your whole being is set to act as if something is so."[3] The consistent study and description of God's character revealed in the Bible and the life of Christ builds a set of beliefs through which the children you serve may be helped to understand the myriad of thoughts, words, attitudes, and actions that bombard them daily.

Ideas For Children To Read The Bible

It is our responsibility, as those who guide children, to help children become familiar with the Bible. As they read God's Word and learn about His ways, they learn to think biblically. The pattern of intentional reading they establish makes God's book the Bible an important part of their life with God.

> "There is a difference between memorizing Scripture and thinking biblically."
> *Tim Hansel*

Children are able to begin to think about the Bible and form a view of the Bible as early as when they are toddlers. Here are two finger plays for toddlers through age three.

The Bible is God's special book (hold Bible)
His Words are written there (open Bible and point to words)
And when I turn each page to look (turn pages)
I handle it with care (hold open in hand)

The Holy Bible is God's book (form book with hands)
Let's open it and see
Where He tells us of His love
He loves you, He loves me (point to others, point to self)

With four- and five-year-olds, hold a Bible in your hands and ask children to hold out their hands, palms up, and together say: "This is God's book the Bible. The Bible is divided into two parts. The Old Testament (touch the Old Testament side and allow children to repeat 'Old Testament') and the New Testament (touch the New Testament side and allow children to repeat 'New Testament')."

Then say: "The names of the first five books of the Old Testament (start with lifting your thumb, and move to forefinger and on through your little finger as you speak) are Genesis, Exodus, Leviticus, Numbers, Deuteronomy. The names of the first five books of the New Testament (on your other hand, begin with your thumb, and move to forefinger through your little finger as you speak) are Matthew, Mark,

Luke, John, Acts." After you say each book's name, allow time for children to repeat the name.

For early elementary age children, add the information that the Bible contains sixty-six books: thirty-nine books in the Old Testament and twenty-seven books in the New Testament. At this age children are able to learn the books of the New Testament by learning the song that gives the names of the books.

For older children, enlarge this activity using both the Old Testament and New Testament. To the Old Testament add the books of history, psalms, proverbs, and the prophets. Add to the New Testament the rest of the books (as it is age-level appropriate).

Elementary age children may be guided to identify that each book in the Bible has chapters and each chapter has verses. The chapters have the big numbers and the verses have the small numbers.

As children become familiar with the structure of the Bible, they also become ready to use it with ease. Their understanding of what once might have appeared to them as a very large book with hundreds of pages changes as they experience that the Bible is many shorter books all bound together into one book.

Make the reading of God's book inviting. Choose Bible versions that are age appropriate. Picture book versions are best for younger children who are not yet reading. *The Beginner's Bible,* published by Questar Publishers, is full of pictures and Bible stories told simply and briefly. *The Jesus Storybook Bible,* published by Zonderkidz, includes delightful illustrations and current, everyday language to describe Bible stories. It is also available on audio CDs.

For older children, choose a children's translation. *International Children's Bible* and *The Children's New Testament*, both published by Word Publishing, are versions children can read and understand. Many older children also enjoy *The Message,* published by NavPress.

Model and practice reading God's book the Bible. Make it a part of the reading habits in your home. As early as first grade, create opportunities at home, Sunday school, or church school for children to read from a Bible. Help them learn how to find a book, chapter, and verse. Start with an easy one such as 1 John 4:16.

> Model and practice reading God's book the Bible. Make it a part of the reading habits in your home.

Encourage the practice of reading God's book the Bible every day with children. A pattern that you might choose to establish is to read portions of the Bible every morning before the day's activities begin. You may be surprised at how children accept this new pattern and even hold you to it.

A friend of mine named Karen established a pattern for morning Bible reading and prayer during a week that she cared for her pre-school age grandchildren in her home. Every day after breakfast, she and the children would go into her home office and sit in the same location "to have devotions." Karen chose to use a collection of proverbs from the Bible especially worded for children in a book entitled *Proverbs for*

Kids from THE BOOK. Several weeks later, the grandchildren came for an overnight visit. As breakfast was about to conclude, Karen suggested they clean up from breakfast and take a walk outdoors. "But Grandma," said the seven-year-old, "did you forget about having devotions?"

Ideas For Children To Observe And Be Informed

This generation of children is asking for a deep, personal life with God. They want to know God, not just with their mind, but also by experience. We need to relate to and teach children in ways that enable them to be "wowed" by God and His ways. The natural world offers us many opportunities.

> We need to relate to and teach children in ways that enable them to be "wowed" by God and His ways.

An intentional strategy to guide children to observe and experience God as they study the natural world is to talk with them about God's amazing creation. Resist just speaking of the knowledge of Genesis creation. Talk about what can be experienced now. Put the "now" and "wow" into the long ago Bible story. (See the "Observation" activity at the end of this chapter for two "wow" experiences.)

Children are natural studiers. By that I mean they are curious, desiring to learn, full of questions, and looking for answers. The natural world provides many examples about who God says we are and of whom we appear to be compared to who we really are. A "butterfly study" is a way to help children be informed about who God has made us to be. (See the "Be Informed" activity at the end of this chapter.)

Children study others by gathering information about them, and then they imitate those they admire. Our cultures' entertainment figures, music, and dress may not be what we want our children to study and imitate, but the fact is they do.

Let this truth motivate you to be a study for your children. As you walk, drive, and move through daily tasks, be aware of what you are modeling. Beliefs, attitudes, emotions, and character are communicated by example.

Be aware of how you are building a sense of belonging, worth, and competence in your children by what you model in your life. I am concerned about our cultures' model and excessive emphasis on self-esteem. When self is built apart from the kingdom of God, then it becomes the kingdom of self. Inform children about self-esteem that is built on a sense of belonging to God because He has chosen to be in relationship with the people He created. Build a sense of worth in your children established from the truth that Jesus died for every individual person. And build a sense of competence that results from the truth that the Holy Spirit is our Teacher and Guide. Then, instead of building self-esteem that becomes a life centered on self, you foster self-esteem that becomes a life centered on humility and grace, serving God, and serving others.

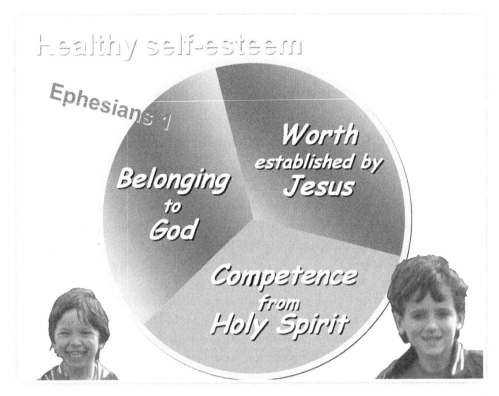

Be intentional to model and live out the truth about our belonging, worth, and competence in thought, word, attitude, action, and practical, everyday experience. An example is the true story of a family I recently observed in a grocery store.

Mother and two children were shopping, chatting as they moved about the grocery store. A customer ahead of them knocked an item off the shelf. The customer failed to stop and replace the item. Without comment, the mother picked up the item and placed it back on the shelf. "Mom, why did you do that? You didn't knock it off," said one of the children. "Replacing the item was a way God gave me to practice being kind and responsible," replied the mom. "And," she added, "it was a way to serve the people here in the store who stock the shelves."

Ways For You To Practice And Model Study

Reflect: Where are you in your own Bible reading patterns? What have you recently observed about God personally as He relates to you? How are you being informed about who God says you are and your own sense of belonging?

Respond: Choose one of the study patterns described in this chapter—Bible reading, observation, being informed. Make a note of your choice. What "new way of thinking" about life and living and life with God do you hope to experience as you practice this pattern of study?

Allow God to change you from within by this way of study. For example, if you choose observation of the natural world, set aside a time to take a walk every day for a week and intentionally observe and be informed by what you see and hear.

Activities And Guided Conversations For Children

Observation

Collect several pictures of caterpillars and sea cucumbers.

Guided Conversation

"Please take a moment to examine these pictures of caterpillars. Do you know that the caterpillars have about 4,000 muscles? How many do you think humans have? (Allow their ideas.) Humans have 629." Then wow them with statistics. "The average caterpillar has 248 muscles in the head segment alone. Why do you think God made caterpillars with so many muscles?" (Allow ideas.)

"There is a study taking place right now to discover how the caterpillar's structure might be duplicated to build a machine with its working parts located in an area as small as the size of a caterpillar. But those involved in the study can't make sense of it yet! I'm convinced that God made caterpillars in a way that unbelieving scientists who dissect them and discover the 4,000 muscles will be baffled and say, 'WOW!'

"Let's observe another idea from the natural world. Take a look at these pictures of sea cucumbers. What does the sea cucumber look like? (Allow their ideas.) The sea cucumber looks like a dill pickle with warts. One variety in particular has one of the best protective abilities of any creature in the ocean. When it is attacked, it poops out its insides, sort of like a snake shedding its skin, and the attacker eats what is left. Wow!" (Fifth and sixth graders love this tidbit because they love to say "poop out" in Sunday school or other such restricted environments.)

Be Informed

Collect several pictures of caterpillars and butterflies.

Guided Conversation

"What do you know about DNA? (Allow answers.)

"How do you know what you know about DNA is true? (Allow answers.)

"Please look at these pictures of caterpillars. What do these pictures tell (inform) you about caterpillars? (Allow discussion.)

"Now take a look at these pictures of butterflies. What do the pictures inform you about butterflies? (Allow their observation.)

"What are the differences between a caterpillar and a butterfly?

"If we asked a biologist to analyze and describe a caterpillar's DNA, he would give us a report that the caterpillar looks like a caterpillar, but scientifically, according to every test including DNA, this green, wormlike being, chomping green vegetation and unable to fly, is fully and completely a butterfly.

"The caterpillar grows into what is already true about it. In the meantime, calling it an ugly worm that does little but eat and telling the caterpillar it ought to be more like a butterfly are not only useless, but they might hurt its tiny ears.

"As it is with the caterpillar, so it is with children, boys and girls, men and women. God has created us to become His children. He has given us the DNA that longs for a relationship with Him. God has created us to be people of compassion, forgiveness, and integrity. He has created us to trust Him and to trust others so that we might care for and serve one another. No matter what we look like right now, His children, formed in His likeness, is who we are created to be."

> God created a caterpillar as a creature that looks nothing like a butterfly but, according to its DNA, is a perfectly complete butterfly with all butterfly behavior and attributes not yet visible. The caterpillar grows into what is already true about it.

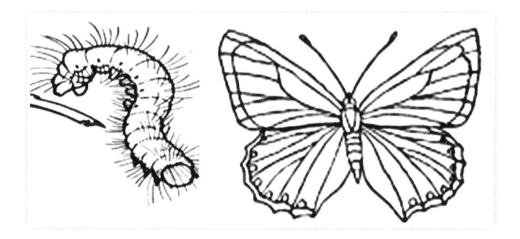

Chapter Four

The Practice of Fasting—Let Go and Take On

I humbled my soul with fasting.

Psalm 69:10, NRSV

Some have exalted religious fasting beyond all Scripture and reason; and others have utterly disregarded it.

John Wesley

When asked if he knew what fasting is, a nine-year-old replied, "Go fast, like on a bike?"

The spiritual discipline of fasting may be a new experience for you as well as for the children you are guiding. Though the practice has a long history, it continues to offer today's followers of Jesus new patterns for living our lives with God.

Biblical Fasting

Biblical fasting is the denial of self in order to sharpen spiritual focus. More than any of the other disciplines, fasting shows us the things that control us. Richard Foster describes another result of the regular practice of fasting. "Fasting helps us keep our balance in life. How easily we begin to allow nonessentials to take precedence in our lives. How quickly we crave things we do not need until we are enslaved by them." [1]

Biblical fasting is most often considered the practice of abstaining from food for spiritual purposes. However, in the context of spiritual and character formation of children in our present culture, this chapter focuses on items other than food that control people.

God's book the Bible provides us with many examples of fasting experiences, the reason for the experiences, and the result.

- *Moses* fasted for forty days and forty nights, twice back-to-back, without food or water. The first was immediately before he received the tablets on the mountain with God. The second was after he came down, saw the Israelites practicing idolatry, and broke the tablets in anger (Deuteronomy 9:7–21).

- *King Jehoshaphat* proclaimed a fast throughout Judah for victory over the Moabites and Ammonites, who were attacking the Israelites (2 Chronicles 20:3).

- *The prophet Joel* called for a fast to turn aside the judgment of God (Joel 1:14).

- *The people of Nineveh*, in response to Jonah's prophecy, fasted to keep their city from being destroyed because of their disobedience to God (Jonah 3:7).

- *The Jews of Persia*, following Mordechai's example, fasted because of Haman's decree to kill all Jewish people. *Queen Esther* declared a three-day fast for all the Jews prior to risking her life in visiting King Ahasurerus uninvited (Esther 4).

- *David* used fasting as an act of humbling his soul (Psalm 69:10).

- *The prophetess Anna*, who proclaimed the baby Jesus to be the Messiah, prayed and fasted regularly in the temple. God allowed her to see the answer to her prayers (Luke 2:37).

- *Jesus* fasted for forty days and forty nights while He was in the desert. During that time, He was tempted by Satan to turn stones into bread and eat them, among other temptations (Matthew 4:2, Luke 4:2).

- *Saul,* later *Paul,* did not eat or drink anything for three days after he was converted on the road to Damascus (Acts 9:9).

- *The people of the church in Antioch* were worshipping the Lord and fasting when the Holy Spirit told them to send Barnabas and Saul for work (Acts 13:2).

- *Paul* and *Barnabus* appointed elders with prayer and fasting (Acts 14:23).

Jesus taught on the outward appearance and demeanor of a fasting person (Matthew 6:16). In New Testament times, fasting was an assumed action of believers (see "And when you pray..." Matthew 6:5 and "When you fast..." Matthew 6:16).

The Practice Of Fasting For Followers Of Jesus

For followers of Jesus, fasting is primarily understood as the choice to let go of something in order to pay attention and hear God. Sometimes fasting is done to focus on another person for help, healing, or decision making. When people fast they choose to abstain from specific things for specific reasons. My child friendly wording for *fasting* is "let go and take on."

Fasting is let go and take on.

The purpose of the practice of fasting for believers today is to help us remember Jesus, seek to become closer to God, and reflect God's nature and character. When introducing this spiritual discipline to children, you may speak of the practice as "*letting go of* patterns and habits (fasting) that do not keep us close to God and His ways and *taking on* (feasting) patterns and habits that keep us close to God and His ways and form His nature and character in us."

The purpose of the practice of fasting for believers today is to help us remember Jesus, seek to become closer to God, and reflect God's nature and character.

Focus On God's Character

Compassion
Forgiveness
Integrity
Respect
Responsibility
Initiative
Cooperation
Perseverance

To model and guide children in the spiritual discipline of fasting (let go and take on), describe concrete ways to take on God's nature and character and let go of destructive vices.

Model and guide your children to make a list of character vices (indifference, revenge, lying, etc.) they would like to begin to let go of (fast) and character virtues (compassion, forgiveness, integrity, respect, responsibility, initiative, cooperation, perseverance) they would like to begin to take on (feast). (A list of character vices versus character virtues and a chart of the foundation virtues and family virtues are provided in the Appendix.)

My suggestion is to practice one virtue per week. Begin by guiding your children to choose the virtue that appeals to them. Compassion is the easiest one. Include a way to focus on God, Jesus, and the Holy Spirit throughout every fasting experience.

The following ideas are examples.

- *Let go of* (fast) being insensitive to others' attitudes and needs. *Take on* (feast) compassion, desiring to help and care for others as well as yourself. Show and give love to people in your family, at school, and in places where you are involved in sports, music, parties, and wherever else you are.

- *Let go of* (fast) thoughts and words that give you the wrong message about yourself. *Take on* (feast) thoughts and words that build your sense of belonging to God. You may memorize this "With-God Life Pledge":

> We pledge to continue to strive to be people who live a "with-God life" that reflects God's character, being and doing
> - the right things,
> - the right ways,
> - for the right reasons,
> - expecting the right result,
> to benefit others and glorify God, according to God's book the Bible.

- *Let go of* (fast) thoughts and words that tell you that you are alone. *Take on* (feast) this prayer as often as possible:

> God, I give You thanks for creating me and loving me. I thank You for Jesus, who teaches me how to live with You. Help me know deep in my spirit that I belong to You and You will never leave me and always love me. In Jesus' name I pray, Amen.

- *Let go of* (fast) blaming, being jealous of others, and wanting to get even with those who have hurt you. *Take on* (feast) forgiveness. Practice forgiveness. Forgiving takes a lot of practice because choosing to forgive may be hard. One of the ways to be a forgiver is to quit blaming yourself and quit blaming others.

- *Let go of* (fast) telling lies, taking what does not belong to you, and breaking promises. *Take on* (feast) integrity. Practice integrity. Talk with God and expect Him to help you mean what you say. People of integrity look for what is true. Ask Jesus to help you know right from wrong. Choose to have truthful, honest thoughts and words, attitudes, and actions.

- *Let go of* (fast) being disrespectful of others and using words that are rude and hurtful. *Take on* (feast) respect. Make it a habit to be polite, using *please* and *thank you*. Be courteous. Open car doors and carry packages for friends and family members.

- *Let go of* (fast) irresponsible attitudes and actions and unwillingness to commit. *Take on* (feast) responsibility. Make it a habit to be personally accountable for your thoughts, choices, decisions, speech, and actions.

- *Let go of* (fast) laziness in thinking and learning. *Take on* (feast) initiative. Take the first step in thinking, learning, being, and doing.

- *Let go of* (fast) opposition, contradiction, and resistance. *Take on* (feast) cooperation. Be willing to serve and work with others to accomplish something that cannot be achieved by a single person.

- *Let go of* (fast) giving up. *Take on* (feast) perseverance. Refuse to give up when things are difficult. Make a habit of following through and finishing what is started.

I know of one church that brings focus to compassion for others by a church-wide letting go and taking on. They have a season before Easter called Celebration of Hope. The focus is on Third World needs. They pack meals for a village for a year through "Feed My Starving Children" (www.fmsc.org). Then they commit to five days of eating oatmeal for breakfast and rice and beans for lunch and dinner with only a small amount of vegetable and meat at one of those meals. This identification enhances the attitude of compassion for those who lack food and water. To raise money to fund the meals they are packing, they drink tap water and invite people to forgo soft drinks and gourmet tea and coffee drinks. When a community comes together for such an event, it enables individuals and families to practice the spiritual discipline of fasting while at the same time become part of something larger than themselves.

Ideas To Model And Guide Children In Fasting

The modeling of fasting is the most effective way to establish this practice in children's life with God. So I encourage you to read on and try to apply some of the ideas presented here for children to your own everyday, walk-around life with God.

> The modeling of fasting is the most effective way to establish this practice in children's life with God.

Fast from media. Together you and your children choose to let go of one or more of the following for one or two days:

- The Internet
- Television
- Radio stations
- Video games
- iPods
- mp3 players
- CD players
- DVD players

Talk about what you might do with your time (read a book, play a board game or a card game with friends or family, take a walk, play outside.)

A friend of mine introduced the practice of fasting to her nine-year-old this way. "Bryce, do you know that Christians sometimes choose to do something called fasting? What do you think of when you hear the word fasting?"

"Go fast, like on a bike?"

"Actually it's the opposite of go. You stop doing one thing so you can do another."

She then gave an example. "An example of fasting would be for me to stop eating dark chocolate for a while, which you and I both love, so I could have a time of being close with God instead. Here's how it would work for me. I would tell myself that whenever I thought about eating a piece of chocolate or had a chance to eat some, I would take a few moments to think about God instead and be close with Him. It would be a way for me to show Him that I love Him."

The Lenten season is a perfect time to introduce the spiritual practice of fasting. Many people understand Lent as a time to choose to let go of things in order to become closer to God. (A Lenten activity is found in the "Activities and Guided Conversations" section in this chapter.)

Children in many parts of our world go without food daily, not by choice, but because there is not enough food. Children in other parts of our world face the growing crisis of childhood obesity and the crisis of bulimia and anorexia among ages 12–18. Both situations are tragic. That said, you may choose to introduce fasting of less healthy foods as a way to guide children into healthy habits of eating and a dependence on the Holy Spirit for wisdom and guidance in developing healthy eating habits. (See "Nutrition" in the "Activities and Guided Conversations" section in this chapter.)

Teaching Tip:

Provide ways for children to make choices to enable them to make healthy decisions.

Practicing fasting first before you invite children to "let go" and "take on" gives you the experience of going through the tough spots. Then you will be less likely to give in to signs of resistance from children. Guide children in what you have discovered.

Ways For You To Practice And Model Fasting

Reflect: Where are you in your own practice of fasting?

Which of the ideas in this chapter appeals to you?

Respond: What would keep you from entering into the practice of fasting? What would motivate you to make a slow beginning? Remember that one of the most effective ways to introduce a spiritual discipline to children is to begin to practice and model the discipline in your everyday, walk-around life.

Pray and ask God for wisdom and discernment each time you enter into a fast.

Write a brief couple of sentences to explain fasting and your reasons for introducing it to your children. Then do it!

Activities And Guided Conversations For Children

Lent

To create a concrete experience for the words *fast* and *feast,* gather items that are well liked by the children you serve. Items could be video games, LEGO® sets, crayons, iPods, or other items popular with children. Fill a see-through container with the chosen items. On separate slips of paper, write numbers, beginning with one, for as many children as you have. Place the folded slips of paper in a container from which the children may draw out a number.

Guided Conversation

"Many people understand Lent as a time to choose to let go of things in order to become closer to God. Lent is the season of forty days from Ash Wednesday until Easter. It is a time to remember Jesus' life and to think about what Jesus' life, death, and resurrection mean to His followers. A special tradition for followers of Jesus during Lent is to let go of some pattern or habit and take on a Lenten promise that helps form a pattern or habit of remembering Jesus' teachings and spending time with God.

"We begin this game by each one drawing a slip of paper. Open the paper to see the number you have drawn. Then look closely at the contents of this container.

"This is a game to give you the opportunity to let go, or fast, from specific items. To have all of the items in this container is to *feast*, or keep all of them. To choose to let go of one or more of these items is to *fast*.

"The number you have drawn tells the order in which each of you will have turn. When it is your turn, you are to take out one item and tell why you choose either to keep the item (feast) or let it go (fast) by putting it back into the container."

Nutrition

Choose to use fasting as a way to teach children about nutrition. Provide paper or a copy of the reinforcement page that follows this activity and pencils, pens, or markers.

Guided Conversation

"To help us practice letting go and taking on (fasting), I have paper and pencils, pens, or markers in order to make two lists. One list is to be for less healthy foods that you would like to try to begin to let go of (fast), and the other list is to be what healthy foods you would like to begin to take on (feast).

"Let's have fun identifying less healthy foods. (Child's name), what is one of your favorite less healthy foods? (Child's name), what is one of your less healthy foods? (Call children by name and suggest that they might choose to add the less healthy foods they identified to their lists. Example: 'Lisa, you said sodas. That would be a good one to place on your list.' Make a short, simple list.)

"Now it is time to make a list of what healthy foods you would like to begin to take on (feast)."

(Repeat the same pattern of calling on children. Then together, choose one item and make a decision about how to accomplish the choice. For example: On Mondays and Fridays, let go of drinks that have sugar in them. Take on water in place of the sugar drinks.)

NOTES: Have some thought-out structure and fun time to replace the food being given up. For younger children, you may choose to lead them to abstain from foods that contain refined sugar. Guide them to make a plan of when and what they could do to let go of a food that contains refined sugar. It might be at a certain meal or specific days that they and you let go of (fast) a refined sugar item such as a cookie. Remember, the choice to "let go of" follows with the choice to "take on." You might guide them to take on (feast) a nutritious item of fruit or nuts.

For older children, you may choose to guide them to let go of (fast) in-between meal snacks one day a week or on a weekend. They may take on (feast) drinking water or juice instead of a snack.

For more specific ideas, see Hess and Watson's book, *Habits of a Child's Heart*[2], chapter three.

Name_____Date _____

Nutrition

Less Healthy Foods   **Healthy Foods**

_____   _____

_____   _____

_____   _____

_____   _____

_____   _____

_____   _____

_____   _____

_____   _____

_____   _____

_____   _____

_____   _____

_____   _____

Chapter Five

The Practice of Simplicity—Live a Simpler Life

Then Jesus said to them, "Be careful and guard against all kinds of greed. A man's life is not measured by the many things he owns."

Luke 12:15, ICB

Simplicity is the only thing that sufficiently reorients our lives so that possessions can be genuinely enjoyed without destroying us.

Richard Foster

Eight year old Jeff in response to a confusing idea: "Keep it simple, silly!"

As I grew up and lived in a Western culture, I subtly came to believe that a successful life would be to have more and more of everything I desired. The discipline of simplicity was not an idea that was presented to me in any of my spiritual, intellectual, or theological studies. In many ways I practiced simplicity as a result of my financial status or my serving in Third World countries. But in recent years, the choosing of a lifestyle to liberate myself from possessions and obligations in order to draw nearer to God has been and continues to be a challenge and a joyful adventure. It also has created a desire to help children establish the pattern of simplicity in their lives at the earliest possible ages.

The Practice Of Simplicity For Followers Of Jesus

For followers of Jesus, the practice of simplicity develops an inward reality that results in an outward lifestyle. Simplicity is not just about economics. It includes a simpler lifestyle that gives freedom from being controlled by possessions, status, time, and energy. In words that children can understand, here is how I define this spiritual discipline. *Simplicity* is "living a life of joyful unconcern from wanting more and more."

> *Simplicity* is living a life of joyful unconcern from wanting more and more.

A careful reading of Scripture on practical, economic questions reveals biblical commands against the accumulation of wealth and the exploitation of the poor. Richard Foster gives examples of biblical challenges to contemporary society's economic values of private property, wealth, attachment to riches, covetousness, and trust in riches:

> The Old Testament takes exception to the popular notion of an absolute right to private property. The earth belongs to God, says Scripture, and therefore cannot be held perpetually (Lev. 25:23). The Old Testament legislation of the year of Jubilee stipulated that all land was to revert back to its original owner. In fact, the Bible declares that wealth itself belongs to God, and one purpose of the year of Jubilee was to provide a regular redistribution of wealth. Such a radical view of economics flies in the face of nearly all contemporary belief and practice. Had Israel faithfully observed the Jubilee it would have dealt a deathblow to the perennial problem of the rich becoming richer and the poor becoming poorer.
>
> Constantly the Bible deals decisively with the inner spirit of slavery that an idolatrous attachment to wealth brings. "Though your riches increase, do not set your heart on them," counsels the psalmist (Ps. 62:10). The tenth commandment is against covetousness, the inner lust to have, which leads to stealing and oppression. The wise sage understood that "Whoever trusts in his riches will fall" (Prov. 11:28).[1]

Jesus spoke frequently to the need for simplicity. "Do not store up for yourselves treasures on earth" (Matt. 6:19). "Watch out! Be on your guard against all kinds of greed; a man's life does not consist in the abundance of his possessions" (Luke 12:15). "Give to everyone who asks you, and if anyone takes what belongs to you, do not demand it back" (Luke 6:30).

Practicing a simpler lifestyle is a difficult task in many current cultures. Here in the U.S., somehow it is wrong to wear clothes or drive cars until they are worn out. Here and in many other countries, every individual, even young children, desires a cell phone. But it is possible to reorient our lives through simplicity so that possessions can be genuinely enjoyed without destroying us. It takes purposeful strategies and practice to keep our focus on choosing a simpler life.

Please don't misunderstand my point. God intends that we have sufficient material provision (see Matthew 6:25–31). There is a proper perspective, however, between people who have insufficient provision and people who spend their lives gathering more than is needed.

It is helpful to recognize that material clutter may lead to destructive spiritual clutter. The stress of time and energy spent on gaining or maintaining a standard of living that is desired and the stress and strain of credit card debt on relationships are contrary to marketing rhetoric on "the good life." It is not true that "the more we have, the greater will be our lives."

> It is helpful to recognize that material clutter may lead to destructive spiritual clutter.

Recently I was told of a conversation between a twenty-something woman and a forty-something woman concerning the purchasing of clothes. The younger lady was excitedly showing her friend her new clothes. The older woman asked, "Which of your present clothing items are you going to give away as a result of these purchases?"

The younger woman replied, "What do you mean?"

"I make it a rule," replied the older but wiser woman, "to give away an article of clothing for each new one I purchase. It helps me be conscious of the need of keeping some degree of simplicity in my life."

The puzzled reply was, "I have never been taught or encouraged to simplify anything."

A friend of mine who is a children's educator and mother said the following about simplicity:

> It's natural to equate simplicity with "stuff" like money, clothes, and toys, but to throw in activities makes it even more challenging because we live in such a busy, driven world. Today's moms face this when they are filling their kids' schedules to the brink! Kids today are not being modeled simplicity.

I find the practice of simplicity difficult but freeing. Difficult because I like gadgets and I like clothes. I like to stay involved in activities and have adventures. But the more belongings and activities I have, the more complicated my life becomes. The practice of simplicity is freeing because I have fewer items and activities to keep track of and more time to enjoy life and focus on relationships with people and with God.

Model Simplicity

Tracy tells a compelling story of how simplicity was modeled for her.

My mother is my model for simplicity. She was a child during the Depression years, and her family of eight children lived with very little, saving and improvising to make the most of everything. She has rarely complained about anything, and I think this is credit for the value she placed on little and sufficiency of what she had rather than focusing on what she did not have. All eight children in this family went from the family farm to college and graduated. Amazing! To this day (she is 84 now), my mom lives very simply and with much contentment and continues to encourage me to live simply by her actions and her gentle encouragement.

Of great concern to me is what we model to our children in response to today's cultural demand that we have and do more and more. The message given to children is that we can never have enough. In *The Hurried Child*, David Elkind writes:

> Parents are under more pressure than ever to overschedule their children and have them engage in organized sports and other activities that may be age-inappropriate. Unhappily, the overtesting of children in public schools has become more extensive than it was even a decade ago. In some communities even kindergarteners are given standardized tests. Media pressures to turn children into consumers have also grown exponentially.[2]

Teaching Tip:

Model and live out spiritual disciplines and character virtues in thoughts, words, attitudes, actions, and everyday experiences.

Children's celebrations are an example of excessiveness. They are driven by the biggest, the best, and outdoing the last celebration. Birthday parties that once consisted of inviting friends for ice cream, cake, and simple presents are now celebrated with clowns, tents, deejays, and extravagant gifts. Graduations, which were once the privilege of those completing high school or college, now begin in kindergarten.

In the mid 1990s, I re-entered the U.S. culture after serving as a teacher and trainer for five years in the former Soviet Union. My culture shock took many forms, but the part that grieved me the most was to see the marketing directed toward children. Here are just a few examples that startled me: the obsession to own the latest Beanie Babies®; the race to McDonald's® for the latest Happy Meal toy; the designer fashions for children; and children's status measured by the school they attend, the sports they play, and their labeled clothing. Something that was amazing to me for all ages was the rise of the "collectables" market. Children's shelves, closets, and lives were filled with stuff!

These days children are driven to collect Webkinz™, described by one site in a quick Web search as "the stuffed animal that comes alive online in Webkinz World." Parents purchase and encourage their children to purchase these toys. The children are then required to spend time on the computer each day caring for them in a virtual world where the children can even buy their toy animals virtual products.

We all have stuff! Many of us hang onto things that need to go: clothes we haven't worn in years, magazines and movies that someone has convinced us need to be saved forever, and books that will never be read or reread. Instead of following the way of the culture, choose to model the habit to give away clothing that is no longer worn. Donate books, magazines, and media items, and borrow these materials from libraries instead of purchasing them. And guide children to establish patterns and habits to do the same.

Focus On God's Character

Compassion
Forgiveness
Integrity
Respect
Responsibility
Initiative
Cooperation
Perseverance

The intentional forming of God's character in you and the children you serve is more than simply directing children to behave in certain ways. It includes equipping children to think, to discern, to ask questions, and to evaluate answers. It requires creating opportunities for children to actively participate in making choices and decisions and to experience the consequences of their choices and decisions.

Practicing the discipline of simplicity creates the opportunity to practice the virtues of compassion, responsibility, integrity, and perseverance. Connect and label the following ideas to one or more of God's character virtues:

- Sort and give items to family members, friends, or those in need. Label this giving as an act of *compassion*.

- Create a field trip. Family or school projects of recycling of cans, newspapers, and other items that can be used again by others are ways to practice the virtues of *compassion* and *responsibility*.

- Eliminate clutter. Label this task as a way to become people of *perseverance*.

- Discuss activities your children are or want to be involved in, and use the discussion as an opportunity to give them encouragement for becoming *responsible* people.

- Make birthday party planning a simpler event. Label for children that having a simpler event requires *responsibility* and *integrity*.

Teaching Tip:

Make it a lifelong pattern to continuously watch for, label, and describe the spiritual discipline of simplicity.

The practice of the discipline of simplicity is a way for us to rediscover meaningful relationships with others, a life less cluttered, the living out of simple virtues, and release from the tyranny of "muchness, manyness, and busyness."

Ideas For Children To Practice Simplicity

Evaluate the ways you are spending time. Time is such a gift. Are you and your children slaves to the clock? Ask the children you serve, "How often do you hear the phrases 'We don't have time to...' or 'I'm so busy' or 'I do not have time to sit and talk'?"

Simplify possessions. Each time you purchase a new piece of clothing for your children, help them give one piece of clothing they have not worn for the past year to a family or charity in need.

Make a field trip to the city dump or recycling center a way to learn now to conserve the world's resources. The recycling of cans, newspapers, and other items that can be used again by others may be a family or school project.

Spend time helping children eliminate clutter. Apply this idea to children's personal spaces in classrooms and at home. Make the cleanout process a low-key, scheduled event. In a school environment, it might happen at the beginning, middle, and end of a school day or before holidays or school breaks. At home, the removal of clutter event might take place on birthdays or before or after family visits. See the "Clutter" activity at the end of the chapter.

Is your community one where each birthday party has to be larger and splashier than the previous one? Then make a difference by returning to a simpler event. Help children think of simpler ways. Perhaps the guests may make their own ice cream sundaes. If it is summer and hot, fill balloons with water for a gentle, benevolent, and fun water fight.

Ways For You To Practice And Model Simplicity

Reflect: What is your first thought and reaction to the idea of simplicity?

Respond: Choose one specific item to give away. Make note of your choice.

What character virtue(s) will help you accomplish the practice of simplicity? Circle one or more: compassion, forgiveness, integrity, respect, responsibility, initiative, cooperation, perseverance.

Model giving away two items of clothing for every one item you purchase or receive.

Activities And Guided Conversations For Children

Clutter

Plan 15 to 30 minutes for this activity.

Guided Conversation

"We are learning to practice simplicity. Let's think and talk about clutter! If one of your friends or family members asked you what the word *clutter* means, what would you say? (Allow ideas.)

"Too many possessions of all kinds may create clutter. How do too many possessions make life burdensome? (Possible answers: hard to find items, easier to find things when there are fewer items and they are organized.)

"What benefit is there when drawers, cubbies, lockers, and closets are cleaned out? (Possible answer: easier to find items.) What might be the logical consequence of things being organized? (Possible answer: time and effort is saved in locating what is wanted.)

"Today we are going to block out some time (15–30 min.) to clean out _____ (define the area). I am setting a timer for _____minutes. See how much you can do."

At the finish of the clean out time, ask children, "What was the hardest part of cleaning out? What was the best part of cleaning out? What is your attitude about clutter now that you have cleaned and organized your _____ (label the area)?"

Activities & Events

Guide a discussion with children about the activities and events (sports, music, tutors, boy and girl scouting, etc.) they are already or want to be involved in. Prepare a place to record children's ideas. Provide paper and pencil, pens, or markers.

Guided Conversation

"We are thinking and talking about the practice of simplicity. To help us identify the activities or events that you and your friends participate in, shout out the names, and we will record the ideas on _____ (white board, PowerPoint, what ever works for your environment).

"Now list on the sheet of paper I have given each of you the activities or events you are involved in. (Allow time to complete this task.) When you have finished, circle your favorites. Why have you continued to do the ones that are not your favorites? (Allow answers.) Which of the activities are you doing to please a parent, teacher, or coach rather than what you truly want to experience? What is keeping you from eliminating any activities you are not passionate about?"

NOTE: At the first opportunity, guide children to discuss with parents, coaches, or other trusted adults why and how they might simplify their life by eliminating their least favorite activities or events.

Simplify Life

Provide a Bible, print a copy of Luke 12:15, or provide the reinforcement page at the end of the chapter for each child.

Guided Conversation

"To guide us in the practice of simplicity, please read with me what Jesus has to say about owning things. *Then he [Jesus] said, 'Beware! Guard against every kind of greed. Life is not measured by how much you own'* (Luke 12:15, NLT).

"Now each of you make a list of the things that you have that are more than you need. (Use the following setup for their lists, or use the reinforcement page.)

Ideas to Simplify My Life

Things that are more than I need:

Things that I want to give away:

"What are some ideas you listed to simplify your life? (Allow sharing.) What are some ideas you listed that are more than you need? (Allow sharing.)

"Who could you phone for a charity pickup? What about an adventure trip to a local charity store or a church deacon closet? What other ideas are you thinking about that would help someone receive the items you wish to give away?"

In an environment where it is possible, help children place the items they choose to give away in a box or bag.

Each time you practice with children the activity just described, label the choice to live a simpler life as "living a life of joyful unconcern for wanting more and more things."

Name_____Date _____

Then he [Jesus] said, "Beware! Guard against every kind of greed. Life is not measured by how much you own." (Luke 12:15, NLT)

Ideas to Simplify My Life

Things that are more than I need:

Things that I want to give away:

Chapter Six

The Practice of Solitude—Spend Time with God

For God alone my soul waits in silence, for my hope is from him.

Psalm 62:5, NRSV

Be still, and know that I am God.

Psalm 46:10

Interaction with a child at a recent Vacation Bible School setting:

Adult: "Would you like to join in the games?"

Child: "No, I just need to sit here and have some time to be by myself."

In this time when everyone, including children, is being encouraged to use Facebook and Twitter on top of everything else going on in their busy lives, solitude must seem a strange idea.

Being alone may create fear in some people. Being alone without noise or entertainment may be uncomfortable. This fear and discomfort drives us to noise and crowds. Our culture capitalizes on these emotions by providing us easy access to a constant stream of music (the louder the better) and words. We attach iPods and iPhones to our ears to insure constant noise. Even when we are on hold on our phones, music or advertisements fill our ears. Many people are so accustomed to noise that it has become a need to immediately turn on a TV or a sound system when entering a room, preventing any time of silence.

Without silence there is no solitude.

The Practice Of Solitude For Followers Of Jesus

Solitude is a basic nutrient of life. Like salt, it draws out the flavor—the flavor of life. Solitude helps us preserve the quality of life and sanity. Solitude allows us to take a step out of the rush, the "hecticness" of life. It restores us to our better self.

Solitude as a basic ingredient of life, like all basic ingredients, needs moderation. Too much solitude is not good and may result in solitary confinement. Too little solitude may result in increased stress, lack of peace, and burnout.

The spiritual discipline of solitude helps us pay attention to God. It is a way of prayer. Practiced regularly, solitude may reverse stress and prevent burnout. My child friendly wording for the spiritual discipline of *solitude* is "spend time with God." Solitude gives times of closeness with God.

> The spiritual discipline of *solitude* is spend time with God.

Solitude And Silence

Psalm 46:10 instructs us to "be still, and know that I am God." It seems that God is strongly saying that it is in solitude and silence that we are more able to hear His voice and be aware of His presence. If you sometimes wonder about God answering your prayers or desire to sense His presence, check the amount of sound and distraction that is present in your life.

> Silence and solitude both work in hidden ways, resembling the work that goes on during winter. In the cold months, it appears nothing is going on. Animals hibernate. Nothing grows. Everything is still and at rest. But in the important sleep of winter, life renews itself. In silence and solitude, God works in ways that are hidden, but nevertheless vital to life.[1]

Some years ago a friend invited me to attend a silent retreat with her. It was a time when I was struggling with issues of relationships and faith. I was sure that what I needed was to be around people I trusted and with whom I could interact. In fact,

I only went to the retreat when my friend agreed that if I couldn't handle the silence, she would leave with me.

The first eight hours were miserable. I couldn't shut off the rehearsal in my mind of the event that had so wounded me. I read my Bible and other materials provided to guide me in solitude and silence. But more than anything, they filled the time until the evening worship. During worship we were able to sing but not speak to one another. Then there was an opportunity to pray. As I prayed, my friend and some of the other leaders came around me, laying hands on me, and I began to weep. They held me for over an hour as I cried out my pain to God, but they kept the silence.

I came face to face with my fear and unwillingness to trust God. I became intensely aware of His presence and was able to rise and return to my room.

For the first time in many days, I slept soundly. Waking the next morning, I discovered that I longed for the solitude and silence to continue, allowing the presence of the Holy One to comfort and give direction and peace. Out of that time came a pattern and basic need in my life—the need to have silence and solitude in the same manner as food, sleep, and relationships with others.

> "Just as the body takes time to recover from an infection that has afflicted it, so the soul needs times of silence and solitude for its recovery from the insane pace of modern life."
>
> *Howard Baker*

The practice of solitude encourages us to have regular times of quiet and stillness in order to hear God speak to us. Often it is easy to shut off the noise outside ourselves—TV, radio, or sound systems—but it is more difficult to quiet the noise in our minds. In the stillness and quiet, our minds race to thoughts of what we need to accomplish in a given day, the phone call we forgot to return, or the e-mails we have not answered.

Solitude and silence do not necessarily take place at the same time. I can be alone, in seclusion, and purposefully listen to music or a recording of Scripture or biblical teaching. Silence is stillness, quietness, calm, and slowing down, which can be experienced in solitude or with others. However, solitude and silence do work together to increase the awareness of God's presence and guidance.

> Solitude and silence work together to increase the awareness of God's presence and guidance.

One way that helps me enter into solitude and silence is to begin to bless or praise the Lord by repeating Psalm 103:1–5 (NRSV):

Bless the LORD, O my soul, and all that is within me, bless his holy name. Bless the LORD, O my soul, and do not forget all his benefits—who forgives all your iniquity, who heals all your diseases, who redeems your life from the Pit, who crowns you with steadfast love and mercy, who satisfies you with good as long as you live so that your youth is renewed like the eagle's.

Another friend of mine uses what followers of Jesus have practiced for centuries to train their minds in quietness, the Jesus Prayer. "Lord Jesus Christ, Son of God, have mercy on me, a sinner." By repeating the passage from Psalms or the Jesus Prayer or both, we can chase away the thoughts and concerns that tend to distract us from the sense of the presence of God and the experience of deep peace and closeness with Him.

The practice of solitude and silence gives us a place of calm and rest from the rush of life. It allows us to hear God's voice giving us direction and help to serve others, to speak the right words to a hurting person, or to know when to be silent and listen to another. It provides a time for God to speak into us His nature and character, guiding us to words and ways to be people of compassion, forgiveness, and integrity.

> The practice of solitude and silence provides a time for God to speak into us His nature and character.

I encourage you to make a space for solitude in your home, classroom, or other living and learning areas. Label this space, and model the use of this space as a place where you and your children may go to practice solitude and silence.

Focus On God's Character

Spiritual and character formation is taking place within every human being throughout life. What is important to those who are followers of Jesus is that this formation results in spiritual and character formation in the likeness of Christ. Remember, the importance of godly character formation is that *character drives conduct.*

Compassion
Forgiveness
Integrity
Respect
Responsibility
Initiative
Cooperation
Perseverance

We know godly character formation is taking place when character virtues of God are lived out when no one is instructing, correcting, or requiring character conduct, attitudes, or beliefs. The logical result of character formation is that the deeds of virtues such as compassion, forgiveness, integrity, respect, responsibility, initiative, cooperation, and perseverance flow naturally—and supernaturally in the likeness of Christ—to others.

Silence and solitude are practiced in my children's spiritual and character formation class. Before the children go to their place of solitude and silence, my teaching team uses puppets whose names, beliefs, attitudes, and conduct reflect specific character virtues. For instance, Carrie Compassion often shares with children about how God is all about compassion. Carrie describes the character virtue of compassion with concrete examples. "Compassion means caring for someone else; to be kind to someone who is sad or hurting, or to show someone that we love them by doing kind things, or by keeping promises. It means we care for our families and our friends, and even for people we don't know. It is a word that means we help others. It is a very big word that means a lot of things."

Carrie then teaches this song (Tune: "Mary Had a Little Lamb").

Have compassion, learn to care,	Have compassion, give your best,
Learn to share, everywhere.	Nothing less, just say, "Yes!"
Have compassion, help someone,	Have compassion, help someone,
God's love and work is done.	Then God's love and work is done.

After the song, children then go to a candle table or kneeling chair for a time of solitude and silence.

One morning, after spending several minutes in solitude and silence, seven-year-old Celie stood up from her kneeling chair, rushed over, and sat next to me. She looked into my eyes with her eyes full of tears and joy and said, "Oh, Miss Vernie, Jesus wants me to be compassionate. He wants me to love and take care of my family and lots of others."

The character virtue of compassion had been the focus of our teaching at that time, and we had experienced it through story and song. In this example, the intentional practice of the spiritual discipline of solitude resulted in a natural—and supernatural—expression of compassion in the likeness of Christ.

Children are capable of an intimate life with God at the earliest ages. Our role is to do our best to guide them to a personal interaction and a relationship with God, His Son Jesus, and the Holy Spirit that results in reflecting God's character and ways. While the character virtue focus in this example was compassion, you may choose to focus on any one of the godly character virtues.

Ideas For Children To Practice Solitude

Children are often thought of as noisy, active, busy people. And they are. We keep them involved in a myriad of activities and events, which meets many of their needs. But children also need times of quiet and opportunities to sense God's presence and hear God's voice. They need to be guided into times of solitude and silence.

Model the conscious decision to turn off the noise. Turn on the car radio or a CD as you might normally do, and then use the intentional strategy of talking with your children about your decision. Say, "I discovered that I automatically turn on the radio when I get into the car, but I would like to practice times of silence and solitude. Let's enjoy complete silence and solitude in the car on this trip. Let's try to quietly think about God being with us today."

Mute commercials when you watch television. This strategy gives three positive results. Children are kept from exposure to the content of advertisements, the volume of commercials is eliminated, and it gives you the opportunity to model enjoying a quiet moment. Enjoying and valuing short times of silence and solitude increases children's comfortableness with silence and solitude. See the "Noise" activity at the end of the chapter.

Another way to help children become comfortable with solitude and silence is to play the quiet game. This game may be played anywhere—in your home, outside on the front lawn, in a classroom, or traveling in a car. The rule is that the winner of this game is the person who doesn't talk until you give a signal (clap hands, ring bell, whistle, or arrive at your destination). Be sure you have the game last as long as appropriate for the age of the children. Ages 4–7: five minutes. Ages 8–11: ten minutes.

Journaling is a traditional way of enhancing solitude and silence. To make journaling attractive for children, suggest they draw pictures and use color to describe their thoughts and ideas.

Another idea is to encourage a time of family solitude on Sunday afternoons. At one time this was a normal pattern to have quiet reflection after church, but Sundays have become as busy and noisy as any other day of the week. One family's Sunday afternoon pattern is for all family members to go to their bedrooms, where they may nap, read, or enjoy a time of quiet reflection. It is an intentional time without computers, music, or television.

Marie Montessori, founder of the Montessori method of education of children, refers to the imagination as something that feeds our spiritual hunger. Imagination helps children in their life with God. They need simple moments of silence to imagine their relationship, world, and life with God. Encouraging children to use their imagination helps them become whole and responsible human beings, creating a life of vision and meaning.

Teaching Tip:

The use of guided conversation helps children focus their imagination on their life with God.

A guided conversation to stimulate children's imagination and enjoyment of a time of silence and solitude might sound like this: "Imagine that you are in your very favorite quiet place. Jesus is with you. Would you like to sit in His lap? Would you like Him to hug you? Imagine what He is saying to you. Imagine what you would say to Him."

Vivian Houk, parent, teacher, and pastor, writes that "the power to produce images in our mind is one of the strengths of the imagination; without it, no faith or religion can really exist. We must imagine the invisible with our mind's eye. This power reminds me of the verse in Hebrews 11 that talks about faith being 'the evidence of things unseen.'"[2] We are capable of producing images in our minds of things that are eternal.

Here's a memorable thought about the spiritual practice of solitude: Our response to life with God is different if we have been taught only a definition of faith than if we have enjoyed sitting in the lap of Jesus and had a conversation about frogs.

Ways For You To Practice And Model Solitude

Reflect: What is your attitude about solitude and silence? What changes have to occur in your everyday, walk-around life to make solitude and silence a priority?

Respond: What is keeping you from practicing solitude and silence—time spent with God? Examine your schedule and choose regular times for solitude and silence.

Model consistent, regular times of solitude and silence until they become lifelong patterns and a habits as common as brushing your teeth.

Activities And Guided Conversations For Children

Noise

Guide children to identify how much noise is in their life at home, classroom, camp, or whatever environment you find yourself with children. To help visual learners, you may choose to provide a copy of the reinforcement page for each child.

Guided Conversation

"We are thinking and learning about the practice of solitude and silence. What ideas come into your mind when you read or hear the word *solitude*? (Allow answers.) The kind of solitude we want to consider is not being alone, or all by yourself. It is having a quiet, alone time with God. It might be a quiet, alone time with God and others.

"Think with me about noise. What noise is in your life at home? How about at school? Traveling in a car? What other places do you experience noise? (Allow ideas.) To help us discover how much noise is in our lives, let's make a list. Use the places you have identified as headings. Then add the kind of noise you hear. Then we may be able to discern how much noise surrounds us each day."

"What have you discovered? (Allow answers.) If you discovered that your environment always has noise from radio, TV, background music, or other sources, what creative, fun way might you choose to have five to ten minutes of silence either alone or each time we are together?"

Guide children to list possible places and times when and where they may have alone, quiet time (solitude) with God. Make note of their choices. Ask the question: "Do you want to start to practice your choice alone, or would you like me or others to join you?"

Solitude and Silence

One activity you may use to introduce children ages 6–9 to a time of solitude and silence is to talk about "hanging out" with God. Help them learn a practice that could be done anytime they wish to "hang" with God.

Guided Conversation

Begin the activity by telling children you are going to describe a way for them to "hang" with God. Use these words:

Make your body still and silent. (Pause and allow children time to do so.)

Breathe slowly and softly. (Pause.)

In the quietness of your mind and body, think with God. Be aware of God's presence with you, in every part of your mind, your body, and your spirit.

Softly sing, "Be still and know that I am God. Be still and know that I am God. Be still and know that I am God."

Picture all the people who love you. Look with God at these people you love. Is there anything special you want to tell God about anyone? Is someone having a birthday? Is someone sick? Is someone doing something special? Is anyone of the people you love lonely? Listen to what God may tell you to be or do. (Pause.)

Now you and God look at the people you love and those who love you, and love them together. (Wait a minute or two.)

Now silently enjoy God's presence and His loving you. (Wait a minute or two.)

End the activity with these words:

Remember, you may have this close time with God whenever or wherever you wish. All you need is yourself and your willingness to be quiet and enjoy God loving you. No one is able to give God your love but you. And no one is able to receive God's love for you except you. It is important for you and God to enjoy each other's company.

What noise is in your life?

To help you identify how much noise is in your life, think and list your thoughts and ideas under each of these headings.

At home

At school

Traveling in a car

Sports practice

Sports event

Music

TV

iPod

Nook

Chapter Seven

The Practice of Submission—Love, Care, and Respect Others

But he gives all the more grace; therefore it says,
"God opposes the proud,
But gives grace to the humble."
Submit yourselves therefore to God.

James 4:6–7, NRSV

Do nothing out of selfish ambition or vain conceit, but in humility consider others better than yourselves.

Philippians 2:3

Submit to one another out of reverence for Christ.

Ephesians 5:21

A child's comment: "I like to be the line leader, but I like to follow a line leader too."

Submission is a really sticky word in our culture, often misunderstood and misapplied. The spiritual practice of submission, chosen intentionally, brings about good in the life of givers and receivers alike.

In the spiritual practice of submission, we surrender to God so that we may more fully give love, care and respect to others. In my child friendly words, *submission* is "giving love, care, and respect to God and others."

> *Submission* is giving love, care, and respect to God and others.

The Practice Of Submission For Followers Of Jesus

The practice of submission enables us to be willing to choose to let God be in control of our thoughts, words, decisions, relationships, attitudes, character, and conduct. The practice of submission also enables a willingness to choose to let another person lead. Submission reminds us that we are not in charge.

> The practice of the spiritual discipline of submission enables the choice to let God be in control of thoughts, words, decisions, relationships, attitudes, character, and conduct. It enables a willingness to choose to let another person lead.

The real issues of submission are the *beliefs* that we are loved by God and belong to Him and the *attitudes* of care, consideration, and respect we have for God and one another. In other words, to the degree that we truly believe God is for us, intimately involved in our circumstances and actively working on our behalf, we will be free from the need to have our own way.

The practice of submission enables us to distinguish between genuine issues and stubborn self-will. If the issue involves theft or anything dishonorable, then one does not submit—it is not stubborn self-will. If asked to be a participant in an idea or event that is not going to harm others or be anything dishonorable and one just does not want to submit to authority or community, then it likely is stubborn self-will. The practice of submission frees us to be the dependent yet empowered children of God and to live for Him, not ourselves.

The best reason for us to consider practicing submission is that submission and servant-hood were the way of Jesus' life on earth. As Jesus submitted to His Father, He served the people around Him. No one was stronger or more submissive than Jesus. In Mark 9:35, Jesus says, "If anyone wants to be first, he must be the very last, and the servant of all." Richard Foster, writing about this verse, says, "The most radical social teaching of Jesus was his total reversal of the contemporary notion of greatness. Leadership is found in becoming the servant of all. Power is discovered in submission."[1]

Jesus lived out this principle of leadership in His interactions with women and children, which not only broke the customs of the day, but also defied class distinctions and declared the worth of all people. The story of His visit with the Samaritan woman at the well is typically recounted as a story about repentance. His submission to sit and talk with her, however, was also a demonstration of Jesus' love, care, and respect for her, a woman living in pain and isolation from society because of her situation.

Jesus' attitude and actions of submission with children were the opposite of His disciples' attitudes and actions. The disciples wanted to send the children away. Jesus' demonstration of love, care, and respect for "the least" was to call the children to Him. He said, "Let the little children come to me" (Luke 18:16). We are called to do the same, not only with women, like the Samaritan woman at the well, and children, like the children Jesus called to Him, but also with others who are counted "the least of these".[2]

Attitudes And Actions Of Submission

Submission and service act in tandem. As we learn to submit to one another, we remind ourselves to stop trying to control circumstances, other people, and events around us. Our beliefs and behaviors toward others' hopes and plans become ones of encouragement and patience. Our attitudes and actions cease to become irritated or upset when some event changes or doesn't go the way we had imagined or planned.

Teaching Tip:

Beliefs drive behavior.

Attitudes drive actions.

The actions of submission are acts of love, care, and respect. These actions often result in receiving a return of love, care, and respect with better outcomes than we may anticipate. A simple example is the respect given when character language such as *please* and *thank you* is modeled and a similar pattern is formed in children. Respect is returned from those to whom it is given.

The practice of submission brings us to a place where power is constantly abandoned in favor of love, care, and respect. Philippians 2:5 says, "Your attitude should be the same as that of Christ Jesus." Submission is more than just actions; it is also the attitudes of Jesus that we are to desire. Henri Nouwen writes that powerlessness and humility "refer to people who are so deeply in love with Jesus that they are ready to follow him wherever he guides them, always trusting that with him they will find life and find it abundantly."³

Awareness Of Submission's Limits

Submission does *not* ask us to give up who we are or lose our personal identity. The spiritual discipline of submission does *not* lead to a loss of our own sense of personhood. Each of us has been created by God as creative, unique individuals with our own gifts, warts, and wrinkles.

> Submission does *not* ask us to give up who we are or lose our personal identity.

Our weaknesses are not evidence that we are of less value than others. Nor do our weaknesses allow others the right to control us. And voluntarily letting others be in control does not mean our own rights as individuals may be violated by them.

Submission has nothing to do with positions in life. God does not intend for His people to be positioned or classed by other human beings, all of whom are as fallible as we all are. "It is a discipline that is not gender-specific or age-specific; we are to submit to each other. Through mutual submission, we are freed to be who we are meant to be and not who position demands we be."⁴

The habit of submission has nothing to do with our becoming doormats with no mind or will of our own. If people willingly give away their personhood and allow someone else to decide and do for them, they may become invisible to themselves and their own sense of belonging, worth, and competence. God intends mutual care, respect, and love for all His people.

Model Ways To Love, Care, And Respect Others

I find it interesting that as human beings we generally like to be in charge. We would rather be in the driver's seat than be driven. We obey the rules of the road—unless we are late or able to "safely" run the yellow light. We may not be aware of a need to control by talking instead of listening. Becoming sensitive to areas where we may surrender our desires in order to benefit others is a goal of submission. Increasing that sensitivity leads us to ways we may live out and model love, care, and respect for others.

Model acts to give up having your own way. Start in small ways in your everyday, walk-around life to give up your desires or what is convenient for you. For example, you have prepared a special dessert for company and discover that your company prefers something quite different. Quietly you put away your dessert and serve what your company desires,

> Start in small ways in your everyday, walk-around life to give up your desires or what is convenient for you.

modeling submission. At an appropriate time, discuss your choice with your children and label the attitude and action as a way to give love, care, and respect. Ask God to increase your awareness of His presence and give you attitudes and actions of submission that reflect His character.

Listen to your tone of voice and become aware of your body gestures when interacting with others. What is your tone of voice when an order is mixed up in a restaurant or a charge is incorrect? When being firm with children, do your tones of voice and body gestures give a sense of security and definition of boundaries, or are they ones of irritation and anger? Be aware as you learn to use calm, joyful, gentle, or kind tones that children often respond with the same tones.

Think about simple, everyday actions in relationship to those around you. Are you able to open a door for another or be the last to choose where you sit at a table? Do you do so regularly?

If your pattern or habit when you grocery shop is to leave your cart in the place where you are parked, begin to return it to the designated cart return area, even if it takes a few more moments of your time. As you do so, label for children that returning the cart is an act of respect and care for the employees of the store. It also gives care and respect for others by preventing the carts from crashing into other cars.

What do you model when another person wrongs you? Children are great observers but often misinterpret what they observe. If your response is arrogant or biting, find a way to apologize. Describe the attitude and action the children observed and your reasons for desiring to respond with understanding and respect. A conversation with children might sound like this: "I apologize for being frustrated about waiting so long at the doctor's office. Being frustrated over something I cannot control is not trusting God to order our day or time."

Use wisdom and discernment as you model and practice this discipline for children. The hope of guiding children in this practice is to build their understanding and attitudes that they are not the center of the universe.

The words we use are important in modeling submission. Teachers and parents may convey and model love, care, and respect by speaking the language of love, care, and respect in their interactions with children.

- "Thank you for closing the door."
- "Please pick up your sweater and books."
- "I appreciate your attitude of patience while I finish my conversation."

Words also model and teach submission by taking children's thoughts and attitudes seriously.

Child: "I don't think it is right to keep the spider in the jar. It doesn't have its freedom."

Parent: "The spider can't be in the house unless it is in the jar. Would you like to keep it awhile and then set it free?"

Notice the parent's response that labels the reason for the rule while modeling submission to the child's needs and desires.

Teaching Tip:

Labeling gives a child a familiar or concrete reason for a rule.

Focus On God's Character

Compassion
Forgiveness
Integrity
Respect
Responsibility
Initiative
Cooperation
Perseverance

Because of the freeing and liberating aspects of valuing other people and giving up our own desires and need for control, the discipline of submission is one of the most important disciplines to govern our relationship with God, family, friends, and community.

Character formation is so enhanced by the spiritual disciplines, especially this one. The modeling and living out of God's character in thoughts, words, attitudes, and actions in practical daily living is essential. Remember, character drives conduct; and the conduct of submission is love, care, and respect toward others.

The character virtue of respect gives the opportunity to honor people by listening and being courteous and polite. Respect enables self-surrender, obedience, gentleness, and empathy for others. Guide children to draw a picture or write some words about these ideas that give respect:

- Spend time with your mother. Examples: hug your mother, help her prepare a meal. Spending time with your mother is a way to give her love, care, and respect.

- Spend time with your father. Examples: play a game, go fishing. Spending time with your father is a way to give him love, care, and respect.

"I have a dream that my children will one day live in a nation where they will not be judged by the color of their skin but by the content of their character."
Martin Luther King, Jr.

- Share something special with a friend. Examples: share a favorite snack, share a toy. To share is to be a person who thinks of others and cares about what they would enjoy.

- Spend time with your family or friends. Examples: play a game together, do chores together. Spending time with family or friends is a way to give them love, care, and respect.

Ask children, "What are some ways you may give people love, care, and respect?"

Ideas For Children To Practice Submission

When people practice love, care, and respect for life, for property, for those in authority, for nature, and for the beliefs and rights of others (submission), they become better friends, better leaders, and better members of their communities.

Have children experience concrete activities that give the opportunity to love, care, respect, and honor others. Guide them to

- listen and be polite.
- let others use their talents.
- obey laws and rules.
- be considerate of others' ideas, attitudes, and actions.

Introduce and memorize Bible words that describe submission. This one, for example, is about love:

Love is patient, love is kind. It does not envy, it does not boast, it is not proud. It is not rude, it is not self-seeking, it is not easily angered, it keeps no record of wrongs. Love does not delight in evil but rejoices with the truth. It always protects, always trusts, always hopes, always perseveres. (1 Corinthians 13:4–7)

Guide younger children with the use of labeling, statements, and questions to practice love, care, respect, and honor with some of the following:

- Draw a picture for someone.
- Say "please" or "thank you."
- Choose to be last in line instead of the leader.
- Share your favorite toy with a friend.
- Carry a package for your parent.
- Choose to stop pleading or whining.
- Come quickly when called by a parent or trusted adult.
- Ask God to give guidance to a family member or friend.

Encourage older children to try some of these actions:

- Tell a person why you respect him or her.

- Teach a younger child to throw a ball.
- Bake cookies to give to someone for no reason at all.
- Write a letter or poem to someone.
- Read a story to someone.
- Use language that encourages others. No name-calling or rude words.
- Attend a friend's sport event and cheer the person on.
- Ask God to give guidance to a family member or friend.
- Obey God's words and ways.

Ways For You To Practice And Model Submission

Reflect:　　What is your understanding and attitude about submission?

In what ways have your understanding and attitude about submission changed as a result of reading this chapter?

How do you presently model submission for your children?

Respond:　　Write down one way you will intentionally model the choice to give up having your own way.

Watch for ways to model and label the giving up of your desires as a pattern and practice of being submissive to God's desire for us to love, care, and respect others.

Model use of words, attitudes, and actions to give love, care, and respect to others. And then be intentional to give children opportunities to do the same.

Activities And Guided Conversations For Children

Respect

The character virtue of respect gives the opportunity to practice obedience, patience, tolerance, and courtesy. Create the following list or copy the reinforcement page at the end of the chapter.

Guided Conversation

"We are thinking about and practicing ways to submit to others with love, care, respect, and honor. I have created a list to help us practice. Next to each action on the following list, circle any statement or action that is respectful. Draw a line through any statement or action that is not respectful. As you work, let me know if you have any questions about any of the statements."

When most of the children have completed the list, guide them through the lines, asking how or why the action is respectful or disrespectful. Examples: "How does saying please honor a person? Why would you care about helping an older person? Why is arguing with parents disrespectful?"

1. Say, "Please."
2. Help an older person carry groceries.
3. Argue and object when your parent says, "It is time for bed."
4. Address adults (teachers, other friend's parents, grandparents, etc.) as "Mr.", "Mrs.", "Miss", "Ma'am", or " Sir".
5. Contradict your parents in public.
6. Treat others the way you want to be treated.
7. Gossip about someone.
8. Say, "Excuse me" or, "Thank you."
9. Talk at the same time someone else is talking.
10. Make others in your presence comfortable.
11. Whisper in front of others.
12. Use words to label the respectful qualities you see in others.
13. Yell at a teammate who makes a mistake in your baseball game.
14. Make fun of someone who has trouble with math or spelling.
15. Argue for truth with dignity and kindness.
16. Use "bathroom language."

NOTE: For younger children, read aloud the ideas that are age appropriate, asking the why and how questions as your read.

Just Imagine

This activity is designed to enlarge the use of children's imagination as well as give them the opportunity to think about how they may open themselves to see God in all people; to serve; and to practice love and care (submission) to people who are different from them.

Guided Conversation

"Close your eyes. Imagine you are a homeless person. You have no home, no family, and no job. You live on the streets. Your clothes are dirty because you do not have a place to wash them. Your pants have holes in the knees. Your shirt or blouse is missing several buttons. Your shoes have holes in the bottom because you walk many miles on pavement. There are holes in your socks. You do not have another pair of socks to replace the socks with the holes. You carry everything you own in a plastic bag. What is in your bag? (Pause for a moment of silent thinking, then continue.)

"It is late morning. You are walking the streets downtown. You need to go to the bathroom. As you try to enter a department store to use the bathroom, the security guard asks you to leave. He is afraid you might steal something. Then you try to go inside a hamburger restaurant. The manager tells you that you can't come in because you might frighten his customers away. What is your attitude now? (Pause for a moment of silent thinking, then continue.)

"You hear that the church on the corner gives food to people in need. You walk up the steps to the big doors of the church and try to open the doors. They are locked. (Pause.) You walk around to the side door where there is a sign that reads 'Office.' It is not locked. You open the door and walk inside. A person smiles and says hello to you. What is your attitude now? (Pause) You tell the person your story and that you are hungry and need a restroom. She directs you to the restrooms and asks you to return to sit in a chair and rest. How does it feel to sit in a comfortable chair in a warm building? (Pause for a moment of silent thinking, then continue.) She returns with a brown paper bag and hands it to you. You thank her and leave. When you are outside, you open the bag. What is inside? (Pause.)

"You sit on the steps of the church near the locked door and eat your lunch. You put the trash back in the bag and carry it to the nearest garbage can. As you continue to walk downtown, it begins to rain. You don't have an umbrella. Where do you go to be out of the rain? (Pause.)

"It is late and the sun is going down. You continue to walk. Now it is dark. You have heard that there is a shelter where people may sleep. You walk some more to find it. Yes, there it is! You see the sign and a line of people waiting to be allowed in. You wait in line. (Pause.) Finally it is your turn to go through the door. A man greets you with a smile and hands you a bag with soap, a toothbrush, a towel, and a wash-cloth. You go to the restroom, wash your face and hands, and brush your teeth for the first time in a long while. What is your attitude now? (Pause.)

"You watch TV for a little while with other people in a big room. Then you go to the cot assigned to you. The cot is in another big room with lots of cots. Some people are sleeping on a mattress on the floor. You are so tired. Your body aches. You are still hungry. You fall asleep. (Pause.)

"A bell rings for everyone to wake up. Someone gives you a cup of coffee and a donut, and you are asked to leave. You are told that you cannot stay at the shelter during the day. So you begin another day walking the streets. (Pause in silence.)

"When you are ready, open your eyes. (Sit in silence for a moment.) What are you thinking? What is your attitude?

"The practice of submission is giving love, care, and respect to God and others. Now that you have imagined how it would be to be homeless, what would be some ways to give love, care, and respect to those who are homeless?

"What would be some concerns if you were to meet and talk with homeless people? Who would you need to help you?"

Name_____Date _____

RESPECT

Next to each action on the following list, circle statements and actions that are respectful. Draw a line through any statements and actions that are not respectful.

1. Say, "Please."

2. Help an older person carry groceries.

3. Argue and object when your parent says, "It is time for bed."

4. Address adults (teachers, other friend's parents, grandparents, etc.) as "Mr.", "Mrs.", "Miss", "Ma'am", or " Sir".

5. Contradict your parents in public.

6. Treat others the way you want to be treated.

7. Gossip about someone.

8. Say, "Excuse me" or "Thank you."

9. Talk at the same time someone else is talking.

10. Make others in your presence comfortable.

11. Whisper in front of others.

12. Use words to label the respectful qualities you see in others.

13. Yell at a teammate who makes a mistake in your baseball game.

14. Make fun of someone who has trouble with math or spelling.

15. Argue for truth with dignity and kindness.

16. Use "bathroom language."

Chapter Eight

The Practice of Service—Become a Servant

Little children, let us love, not in word or speech, but in truth and action.

1 John 3:18, NRSV

Everybody can be great, because everybody can serve. You don't have to have a college degree to serve. You don't have to make your subject and your verb agree to serve ... You don't have to know Einstein's theory of relativity to serve ... You only need a heart full of grace, a soul generated by love.

Dr. Martin Luther King Jr., "The Drum Major Instinct"

Overheard, two young children discussing what to play: "Let's pretend we are waiters. We can offer drinks and help people choose food. We can bring their food and ask if there is anything else they would like. Then we can do the dessert thing. It is fun to serve others."

Often service is thought of in terms of an occasional commitment that takes a small part of a day or a week or perhaps a month. The spiritual discipline of service is so much more. It is service not only to those around us, but also to the Lord. To become a servant to others is less a task or series of tasks than an attitude of obedience to love and care for the people in our communities and around the world. In serving others, we serve the Lord.

The Practice Of Service For Followers Of Jesus

Attitudes drive actions! Richard Foster describes how to form a positive and appropriate attitude about service.

> Do everything you do, especially the lowest and most menial of tasks, with an attitude that you are serving the Lord. Whenever possible, look for additional ways to serve or to lighten another's burden. If you can perform your service without notice, all the better.[1]

Spiritual disciplines help us center on God, be aware of the presence of God, and become less preoccupied with ourselves. My child friendly wording for the practice of *service* is to "become a servant to all."

The practice of service—to become a servant— at the earliest possible age builds lifelong attitudes, patterns, and habits of being aware of the needs of others and a willingness to serve all, including the least. Helping children care for and be aware of people's needs beyond their backyard is one more way for us and for our children to love God.

> The practice of *service* is to become a servant to all.

Service And Humility

Humility is one of those virtues formed in followers of Christ through forgiveness, and it is worked into our lives through the spiritual practice of service. To believe we have acquired humility is evidence that we haven't. Humility is never gained by intentionally seeking it. Instead, it is formed in us and becomes part of our character as we find ways to intentionally be a servant to others.

The choice to become a servant is the most helpful way to promote the growth of humility. Foster describes the choice. "When we set out on a consciously chosen course of action that accents the good of others and is, for the most part, a hidden work, a deep change occurs in our spirits."[2]

William Law in his book, *A Serious Call to a Devout and Holy Life,* speaks of every day being a day of humility as we learn to serve others. If we desire to be people whose actions are driven habitually by humility, Law counsels us in this way:

> Condescend to all the weaknesses and infirmities of your fellow-creatures, cover their frailties, love their excellencies, encourage their virtues, relieve their wants, rejoice in their prosperities, compassionate their distress, receive their friendship, overlook their unkindness, forgive their malice, be a servant of servants, and condescend to do the lowest offices to the lowest of mankind.[3]

Jesus models a classic example of serving with His disciples. "Jesus knew that the Father had put all things under his power, and that he had come from God and was returning to God; so he got up from the meal, took off his outer clothing, and wrapped a towel around his waist … and began to wash his disciples' feet" (John 13:3–5).

He responds to His disciples' question about this act by saying, "You do not realize now what I am doing, but later you will understand" (John 13:7). Often our serving others brings a similar response. People are not always comfortable receiving from others. An essential condition of service is that we keep our eyes focused on God, not the immediate outcome.

There are things in life that must be done. I call them the "maintain-ness" of life. Menial tasks such as scrubbing of the pasta pan or cleaning the bathroom, accomplished with the attitude of serving those we love, give ample opportunity for this practice.

Focus On God's Character

Godly character formation is accomplished as we surrender to the Spirit of God to form His character in us. An important part of our continued growth in godly character formation is the patterns and habits of offering service to God and to others.

Foundation Virtues:
Compassion
Forgiveness
Integrity
Respect
Responsibility
Initiative
Cooperation
Perseverance
Family Virtue:
Humility

Earlier chapters have focused on the character virtues of *compassion, forgiveness,* and *integrity,* three of what I label the "foundation virtues."[4] The practice of service, through love and care for people in their communities and around the world, certainly continues the formation of these three virtues. And as this chapter points out, the practice of service adds the virtue of *humility* to that list. Humility is what I label a "family virtue" of the foundation virtue of forgiveness.[5]

In addition, the practice of service increases the formation of *respect, responsibility*, and *initiative*. Children need help in recognizing these virtues in their lives. Make an intentional pattern to continuously watch for, label, and describe firsthand experiences that are examples of these virtues.

Respect is showing honor to people by listening, being courteous and polite, and demonstrating manners. It includes self-respect, the avoidance of excessive self-criticism, and respect for order and authority.

> Humility is formed in us and becomes part of our character as we find ways to intentionally be a servant to others.

Responsibility is the personal, individual acceptance that every human being is accountable for his or her behavior, including thoughts, attitudes, choices, decisions, speech, and actions.

Initiative is choosing to take the first step in thinking, doing, or learning. It includes being responsible for follow-through. Initiative is demonstrating responsible thoughts and actions without being prompted or without being influenced by limited choices.

Use guided conversation to label a virtue as you and your children practice the discipline of service. "Kyle, noticing that Mrs. Allen could use help to carry her groceries into her house was a responsible thing to do. You are becoming a responsible person."

Ideas For Children To Practice Service

Remember children need to learn about relationships. Serving others helps children learn how relationships are formed and maintained. You are their guide and teacher. Use firsthand experiences and teachable moments to talk with them about how they like to be treated. Have conversations about how God and others might like to be treated in similar ways.

Teaching Tip:

Because children think concretely, firsthand experiences and teachable moments give opportunities to gain understanding and build positive attitudes.

Recently in the area where I live, a forest fire destroyed hundreds of homes. While I was caring for my eight-year-old grandson, we had the following conversation about a firsthand experience in a teachable moment.

"You know, Josh, you lost your favorite lunch box today," I said. "You may find it, or perhaps you may need to replace it. Think about the people who have lost their homes in the fire. How do you think they may want people to treat them? What might we be able to be or do for them?"

"I bet they are glad when people bring them stuff to replace what they lost," Josh replied. "Maybe we could go and buy something they need."

This story is an example of guiding children to be aware of the needs of others and how they would like to be treated. Guiding children in the practice of service to others also includes helping them learn how to use words that are respectful, how to give and receive, and how to recognize when to apologize and why. When a joyful attitude is nurtured along with patterns and habits of becoming a servant, an attitude and character virtue of humility begin to form.

An important part of guiding children in the practice of service is to model receiving acts of kindness and words of compliments graciously. When children receive a compliment, guide them to respond with a sincere "thank you" and enjoy the affirmation. Receivers are needed to enable giving. Many find receiving more difficult than giving. Receiving graciously is another attitude that enables the forming of humility.

> An important part of guiding children in the practice of service is to model receiving acts of kindness and words of compliments graciously.

Encourage ways for children to help you, to help each other, and to help people with obvious needs. At mealtimes, make it a pattern that children as well as adults remove their plates as they leave the table after a meal. "Thank you for taking your plate and utensils to the kitchen counter." The youngest child is able to begin this pattern by removing his or her fork, knife, or spoon. Plates and cups can be added as the pattern is developed.

Make the purpose of household chores the practice of serving one another. Use guided conversation to encourage siblings to help each other make their beds, pick up their rooms, and put toys away when finished playing. "Making beds is easier when you serve each other by making your beds together." If you choose to pay children for some chores with the hope of establishing the importance of a work ethic, make a clear set of chores that are done in order to earn money and another clear set of chores that are done to serve members of the family, neighborhood, and community. In classroom settings, encourage children to help each other gather and put away materials and equipment.

Model an awareness of needs in your neighborhood or classroom. "Mrs. Jones next door just arrived home with a car load of groceries. Let's go help her carry groceries into the house." Other choices would be to shovel snow from the sidewalk, or pick up trash that is blown or thrown into the yard. Open and hold doors for others. I especially encourage dads to model these behaviors for their children and guide children to do the same. In many modern cultures, the opportunity for young men to experience the attitude and actions of service is lacking.

Recently my husband opened a car door for me. One of the other passengers remarked, "Does he still open the door for you?" I responded, "Yes, that is who he is, a gentleman who serves others. He not only opens and holds doors for others, he also rises when a lady gives his seat to women and mothers with children."

Be intentional about serving one another in the environment where you are interacting with children. Inform children when someone they know is in the hospital, and help them prepare a get-well card. Label these opportunities as ways to serve the people in your community.

Search for projects for which there is no personal benefit. Try some projects that are things you like to do as well as ones that are new or may seem somewhat difficult. Service project ideas that children may accomplish as a family, in a classroom, or as a larger church or school event include the following:

- Prepare school bags for children to be given as donations in your community at the beginning of the school year.

- Take a trip to the grocery store to purchase food items for families with new babies, people recovering from illness, or shelters and food banks.

- Make "Surprise Bags" filled with hygiene or school supplies to give to homeless shelters and people who live on the streets or in Third World countries.

- Grow flowers and houseplants with the purpose of creating bouquets to give to others to express love or respect or to bring joy to someone who needs cheering up.

- Pick up litter. It may not be the most attractive project, but it does increase the understanding of the reason for not littering. Provide bright colored latex gloves and various sizes of trash bags appropriate for the ages of the children involved—small for small children, middle size for middle size children, large for large children.

Ways For You To Practice And Model Service

Reflect: Where are you in your attitude and practice of obedience to love and care for the people in your communities and around the world?

In serving others, we serve the Lord. In what ways have your understanding and attitudes about the discipline of service increased or changed as a result of reading this chapter?

Respond: Today think about a way you can serve those who are not able to work or support themselves. Serving might be anything from visiting or making a meal for someone who has lost a job, recently had a baby, or is recovering from a surgery. Make a note of what you hope to do and what it will take to accomplish your choice.

Activities And Guided Conversations For Children

Tithe Money

Guide children to begin lifelong patterns and habits of tithing their money, time, and talent as part of the practice of service. A tithe is ten percent of something. Guiding children to give a tenth of their money, time, and talent can become a beginning and concrete way for children to form a one hundred percent attitude of service. This activity and the "Tithe Time" activity are designed to be used sequentially.

Provide ten pennies, ten dimes, and one dollar to each child to manipulate, or use Cuisenaire® Rods if available.

Guided Conversation

For younger children

"We are learning about the practice of service. One way God's book the Bible guides us to serve is to choose to give a tenth of our time, talent, and money.

"First we are going to discover what is a 'tenth'. I am giving each of you ten pennies. Count them with me. Here is a dime that is the same as ten pennies. One penny is a 'tenth' of a dime. Here are ten dimes. Count them with me. Ten dimes are the same as one dollar. A dime is a 'tenth' of a dollar."

For the use of Cuisenaire® Rods

"Here are ten red rods that are the same. Line them up end to end. Count them with me. Here is a yellow rod that is the same as ten red rods. Place the yellow rod next to your line of red rods. What do you observe? Ten red rods are the same as the yellow rod, or a red rod is a 'tenth' of a yellow rod. Here are ten yellow rods. Line them up end to end. Count them with me. Here is a green rod that is the same as ten yellow rods.

Place the green rod next to your line of yellow rods. What do you observe? Ten yellow rods are the same as the green rod, or a yellow rod is a 'tenth' of a green rod."

For older children

Discover what they know about a tenth by asking, "How many pennies are in a dime? (Allow answers.) How many dimes does it take to make a dollar?" If needed, guide them through the exercise for younger children.

For younger and older children

"Now that you understand what is a tenth, we are going to think about tithing money. How may you determine what money you have belongs to you personally and what would be a tenth of that amount? Choose to put your tenth into a container of some kind, a jar or piggy bank, to spend only to help care for someone or support a need. Some opportunities to spend your tithe would be to help with the expenses of your Sunday school class and church. What are some other ways your tithe of money might be used?" (Possible answer: purchase food for a food bank or appropriate toys or gifts to take to a children's hospital.)

Tithe Time

As children's concrete understanding of a tithe increases, introduce the idea that a portion of the time they have to spend also becomes a service to God and others. Ten percent of their time, intentionally planned and used to serve God and others, creates the practice and habit of tithing their time, which in reality amounts to much more than a tenth. Use a calendar as a concrete activity to introduce the practice and habit of tracking their everyday time. Provide a blank calendar for each child.

Guided Conversation

"We are learning about tithing as a way to practice serving. We explored the idea of tithing our money to be used to serve others. Now let's think about ways to tithe our time to practice serving. I am giving each of you a calendar to write your daily events in one week of your life.

"What word might you write on each day? (Monday–Friday.) What picture or symbol could you draw in each day to show your meals? You might think of creating different drawing ideas for each of your daily meals.

"What events take place on each day or every week? (school, music lesson, sports, Sunday school, church, etc.) Circle which events build the attitude of obedience to love and care for the people in your home, neighborhood, school, church (community), and around the world."

NOTE: Help young children include times when they talk with God, hold very still while mother or father washes their face, put away toys, bring the newspaper into the house, and chat with grandparents. Help older children include times when they care for siblings, shop for groceries, and deliver food to a soup kitchen or a friend or neighbor who needs a meal.

Next, guide them to determine if they are spending at least a tenth of their time to love and care for the people in their lives. You and your children may be surprised by what you discover. These two concrete activities—to give a tithe of money and to give a tithe of time—can lead into an examination of ways to tithe the talents that God has placed within each of us.

Tithe Talent

For each child, make a list of possible talents, or copy the list of talents at the end of this chapter. Also provide a copy of the reinforcement page to identify people in the neighborhood.

Guided Conversation

"We are learning about tithing as a way to practice serving. We explored the idea of tithing our money and our time to be used to serve others. Now let's think about ways to tithe our talents. Talents are special or outstanding abilities. Take a look at this list of talents and add any other talents either you or your friends have. (Pause.)

"Underline the talents that you have. Then star the ones that serve God by loving and caring for the people in your life. Are you using a tenth or more of your talents to serve God by loving and caring for the people in your life?"

Now guide children to identify people in your neighborhood or community who are not able to work or support themselves. There is a reinforcement page at the end of this chapter to help to enable this identification.

"Is there anyone in your neighborhood or any of our friends that are not able to work or support themselves? Here is a page to help you identify people in your neighborhood or community who are not able to work or support themselves. Print your ideas on the lines provided.

"Now let's ask God to help us think of ways we might be able to love and help them. (Invite children to a moment of silence and then to pray, asking God for ideas.) What are some of the thoughts or ideas you have now that we asked God for help? Print your ideas on the lines provided. What is needed to accomplish some of these ideas?"

When children's acts of service have been completed, ask children to draw or write what was the best part of serving and what was the hardest part of serving.

Name_____Date_____

Talent List

Play a musical instrument

Sing

Write

Draw

Learn math and science

Listen

Guard the reputation of others—refuse to speak unkindly of others or allow others to speak words of harm about others

Use common courtesy—words of "thank you," "yes," and "please" and thank-you notes

Be hospitable—invite a friend to join in an activity or visit your home

Receive acts of kindness and words of compliments

_____

_____

_____

People in my neighborhood or community who are not able to work or support themselves:

_____

_____

_____

_____

_____

"Please, God, help me think of ways I might be able to love and help them."

Some of the thoughts I have as I ask God for help:

_____

_____

_____

_____

_____

_____

Draw or write what was the best part of serving and what was the hardest part of serving.

Chapter Nine

The Practice of Confession—Tell the Truth

If we say that we have no sin, we are fooling ourselves, and the truth is not in us. But if we confess our sins, he will forgive our sins. We can trust God. He does what is right. He will make us clean from all the wrongs we have done.

    1 John 1:8–9, ICB

Therefore confess your sins to each other and pray for each other so that you may be healed.

    James 5:16

A child of the light confesses instantly and stands bared before God; a child of the darkness says, "Oh, I can explain that away."

    Oswald Chambers

"I confess, my brother did it!"

The spiritual discipline of confession is not at all easy when we first begin to practice it. As the child's comment above demonstrates, it is easier to confess what others have done than it is to confess the truth about ourselves.

The Practice Of Confession For Followers Of Jesus

At the core of the practice of confession is the telling of truth, but some present day cultures teach us to look for a way to explain away *Confession* is telling the truth. our attitudes and actions or find ways to blame someone else for harm done. It is somehow more acceptable to exaggerate or tell a lie to cover up what we have thought, said, or done wrong rather than to confess what is true. My child friendly wording for *confession* is "telling the truth."

In 1 John 1:9, the apostle John connects truth and our sinful nature: if we are truthful with ourselves, we know that we all think, say, and do wrong (sin). In the context of speaking about the consequences of sin, Jesus states that "everyone who sins is a slave to sin" but "the truth will set you free" (John 8:32–34). Life with God enables us to become truth tellers.

God's desire is always to give and to forgive so that we may be in a right relationship with Him. God's sacrificial gift of His Son Jesus demonstrates His love and great desire to forgive us. Through this gift, God made confession and forgiveness possible. And through confession and forgiveness, we experience healing and the transformation of our mind, will, and spirit towards Christlikeness.

In her book, *Spiritual Disciplines Devotional,* Valerie Hess describes confession.

The discipline of confession is not about appeasing an angry God who will send us to hell if we don't behave. The discipline of confession is about a loving Heavenly Father who wants the best for us and is willing to heal us if only we will honestly admit that we are in need of healing. God invites us to come to a place of deep remorse for our sin-filled thoughts, words and deeds. And God in his infinite mercy understands that sometime it may take us a while to get to that place. Sometimes we can only confess bits and pieces of the sin as we let God have his gentle yet thorough ways of cleaning house in the dark recess of our minds and hearts. As we come to confession, we are invited to be as honest as we can be at that moment, trusting that God will bring the healing and release we need.[1]

When I was five years old, my family lived on a block with just three houses. My house was the middle house. On the south end of the block was a restaurant with a parking lot. On the north end were three business establishments with a sidewalk that formed a square in front of the stores. I was allowed to ride my tricycle to the south only as far as where the restaurant parking lot began, but I could go all the way to the north and ride around the square walkway and back to my house.

Mr. and Mrs. Black were the owners of the drugstore that sat at the farthest end of the block. They knew my family and my brother and sister by name. I would often ride my tricycle down, go into to the store, and just say hi.

One day I saw a display of Hershey's® almond chocolate bars. As I went by it, I was sure I heard a chocolate bar say, "Take me." I said hello to Mr. and Mrs. Black, and as I passed the display, I took a Hershey's bar. I jumped on my tricycle, road to my house, went around to the back porch, opened the candy, and enjoyed eating the whole bar. I then heard the phone ring. My grandmother answered.

"Well, hello, Mr. Black. How nice to hear from you," she said. Oh my, I knew right away why Mr. Black was calling. Grandma's next words were, "Verneal (that's my full name) will be right down, Mr. Black. Thank you for calling."

Grandma sat down beside me and told me that Mr. Black had seen me take the candy bar. She said, "Mr. Black and I both care for you too much to let you become a person who steals from others." I began to cry and tell her that I knew it was wrong to take the candy bar and how sorry I was for taking it.

"It is wrong to take something without paying for it," she said in response, "but you may make it right by telling him the truth and paying him for the candy bar."

Grandma wiped my tears, helped me take the correct amount of money out of my piggy bank, and walked me to the front door. "You're coming with me, aren't you, Grandma?"

"No, Verneal," she replied. "You took the candy bar by yourself, you ate it by yourself, and now you may make this right by yourself. I will stand here and watch if you need help, and I will be here when you come back to hug and thank you for doing what is right."

I thank God that my grandmother guided me to tell the truth (confession) and also to do what was needed to correct what I had done wrong.

Learning to speak and tell the truth is an integral part of forming the pattern and habit of confession. In this situation, I might have just confessed to my grandmother that I did take and eat the candy bar, but my wise grandmother understood there was more. It would have done me little good as a child if I had been allowed to tell only grandmother the truth without the opportunity to correct the wrong.

The spiritual practice of confession forms best in us when we take appropriate, concrete actions to keep us from doing the same wrong again. I still remember my tears of shame and the burning in my cheeks as I told Mr. Black the truth. The experience was a memorable step that kept me from committing the same mistake again.

What happens when you make a mistake? Does God change His mind about you?

God never changes His mind. God is not shocked. He may be sad. But because God loves, God gives grace and forgiveness. Our task is to respond to our mistakes with humility. "You're right, God. I agree with You that what I have thought or said or done is wrong. What do You want me to learn from my mistake? What do I need to be or do differently?"The result of our being truthful with Him is the formation of teachable and humble attitudes in us.

Focus On God's Character

Foundation Virtues:
Compassion
Forgiveness
Integrity
Respect
Responsibility
Initiative
Cooperation
Perseverance
Family Virtues:
Trust
Humility

God longs for us to be formed into the loving character of Christ. Godly character formation is all about obedience, practice, and choices that allow God's Spirit to form the character and likeness of Jesus in us. It requires our effort—through individual choices, beliefs, attitudes, language, actions, and obedience—to cooperate with the work of God's Spirit.

Four qualities of God's character are closely linked to the practice of confession: integrity, trust, forgiveness, and humility.

- *Integrity*—see ourselves as God sees us—our true identity.
- *Trust*— start with trusting who God says we are. Trust God's grace and mercy.
- *Forgiveness*—receive and give. No more blame.
- *Humility*—"You're right, God. I agree with You and trust You with what I have confessed."

Integrity leads to confession, and confession leads to change and to become the people God wants us to be. To be a person of integrity is to act out of the truth of who you are as a child of God, to see and know yourself as God sees you. Living out the identity that God declares for you includes knowing that you are: a child of God (John 1:12); Christ's friend, bought

> Integrity leads to confession, and confession leads to change and to become the people God wants us to be.

with a price (1 Cor. 6:19–20); a saint (Eph. 1:1); salt and light of the earth (Matt. 5:13–14); free forever from condemnation (Rom. 8:31–34); and a minister of reconciliation for God (2 Cor. 5:17–21). Living out your identity as a child of God also means you cannot be separated from the love of God (Rom 8:35–39); can do all things through Christ who strengthens you (Phil. 4:13); belong to God (Col. 3:12); and much more! We need to see ourselves and one another as saints who sin rather that as sinners who are saved.

We can act out of the truth of who we are only when we trust who God says we are. Trust lays the foundation for maturity and the freedom to hear the unconditional call of God's love to confess our sins. Often we compromise our integrity because we want to look good instead of telling the truth.

Confession allows the formation of forgiveness and humility. Individually, when people experience forgiveness, they are freed from guilt and feelings of failure. When people practice forgiveness in community, they break the cycle of revenge. Forgiveness makes it possible for people to stop blaming and to choose to stop being angry toward those who have hurt or wronged them.

To confess, humbly acknowledge, and agree with God that what is thought, said, or done is hurtful and wrong and to receive and give forgiveness result in the formation of teachable attitudes and character virtues. Here are three simple statements for children to practice to make a concrete confession.

- "Lord Jesus, what do I need to do differently?"
- "Help me learn from my mistake."
- "I want to be and do what You, God, want me to be and do."

Guide Children To Understand Confession

Begin at the earliest ages to build a child's understanding of the word *confess* as a positive way of saying what is true. "I *confess* that Jesus is God's Son. I know it's true." "I *confess* that God loves me. The Bible says it is true." "I *confess* that I belong to God. It's true." "I *confess* that I am Jesus' friend. It is the truth." This beginning enables you and the children you serve to develop positive attitudes about talking with God about truth. It is much easier to learn to confess truth than wrong. Just as important, this practice develops a positive attitude about truth and talking with God concerning the truth about the wrong things that are thought, said, or done.

> Begin at the earliest ages to build a child's understanding of the word *confess* as a positive way of saying what is true.

To confess is *also* to agree with God that what is said, thought, or done is not what God wants. This aspect of confession is also one you want to guide children to make a lifelong habit. Model it for children. An example might be: "Wow, I agree with you, God, that I really had an attitude attack about my neighbors' trash blowing into the yard. Please help me change my attitude toward my neighbors and find a way to be helpful with their trash when the wind blows and they are not aware of the location of their trash."

Ideas To Model And Guide Children To Practice Confession

The discipline of confession—telling the truth—must become a part of your everyday, walk-around life. Your life with God. As with all the disciplines, modeling is the most effective way to teach and guide your children into this practice.

Become comfortable with expressing genuine regrets for attitudes and actions to your children. You may need to practice statements such as: "Jason, slamming the door and yelling at you when I was angry was wrong. The truth is that I am tired, and anger is not the way to bring me rest. I hope to avoid making this mistake again."

Confession may be a new idea to some children. They need your encouragement. Children need to know that it is okay to tell the truth about (confess) their attitude attacks and inappropriate actions. They need to be encouraged to be remorseful about words, attitudes, and actions that are hurtful and destructive to themselves and others.

> Children need to know that it is okay to tell the truth about (confess) their attitude attacks and inappropriate actions.

One of my friends tells how she and her family model and guide conversation to practice confession at dinnertime.

Tonight we practiced confession at dinner. We don't do it every night at dinner, but when I sense the girls are feeling tension while we are eating, I might say, "Let's think about our day. Can you think about a time today when you might have hurt someone with your actions or your words?" This question is very concrete. Even Anwen, who is six, understands.

We don't really "allow" saying ways that people hurt *us*. (Doing so would very quickly descend into tattle-telling.) That conversation is for another time. Instead, we think about when we have hurt *others*. We discuss how to say we're sorry, and if the person we hurt is at the table, we say we're sorry right then. Adults participate too. In fact, tonight I confessed that when I was with my mom today, I babbled on and on and didn't even listen to the things she wanted to say. I was selfish.

When we're done sharing, we thank Jesus for helping us to admit when we have done wrong, and we ask Him to help us to love one another instead of hurting one another. The whole experience is very conversational and relational.

After you guide children into positive attitudes about telling the truth, be intentional at least once a week to model one or two of the following suggested activities to help in the practice of this discipline.

- Ask God to forgive you for something you thought, said, or did wrong. Name the specific attitude or action. Thank God for being with you and helping you be aware of the wrong. Thank Jesus for making it possible to be forgiven. Ask the Spirit of God to continue to be your helper and guide you to ways you may right the wrong.

- Apologize to children whenever you lose your temper or your words, attitudes, or actions are wrong. Wrap your arms around young children as you tell the truth (confess). "It is wrong to be this upset over _____. I love you, and I am sorry for my hurtful attitude."

- Pray for someone who annoys or irritates you. Confess your attitude and actions in the situation. Then pray for that person and ask Jesus to help with a solution to the problem.

- Practice thinking certain ways. Reject negative thoughts or sinful thoughts as soon as you become aware of them. Don't hide them. Confess them to Jesus and leave them with Jesus. Practice thoughts of trust, gratitude, and thankfulness so these thoughts become more prominent and natural.

Teaching Tip:

Children's thinking is limited by their perspective.

Remember that children's thinking is limited by their perspective. A friend recently told me that as a child she was fearful to admit to doing wrong because when she was caught doing wrong, she was always told, "Shame on you! You should be ashamed of yourself!" So her perspective was that telling the truth was dangerous and hurt. This story demonstrates the importance to continuously build positive attitudes about telling the truth.

Telling the truth, confession, leads to the opportunity to build the attitude and action of forgiveness. Many times children are taught forgiveness by being instructed to say, "I'm sorry." In reality, this action is repentance. Forgiveness happens when people first agree with God that they have thought, said, or done something He does not want them to think, say, or do. For children, forgiveness starts with agreeing with a significant adult in their life or the authority figure in a situation that a wrong has occurred (telling the truth).

Here is an example. An adult speaks with a child: "You took Brianna's bike for a ride without asking her permission." The child responds, "Yes, it was wrong to take the ride without asking Brianna's permission." An indication of the child's understanding of this part of confession and forgiveness is the child's ability to say, "I was wrong." It is usually easy for a child to say "I'm sorry," but often children are initially unwilling to admit they are wrong. Guide a child to say "I was wrong" rather than only "I'm sorry."

Here is another example from a parent.

> I model confession mostly when I apologize to my kids when I have clearly lost my temper, misjudged a situation, or made assumptions that were not mine to make. I ask their forgiveness, and I ask them to pray with me as I ask for forgiveness from God. I teach the discipline as "life happens." Confession is best taught through the situation, nearly from the moment of our birth, because we demand our way and hurt those around us. Humility and acknowledgement are the only known cures.
>
> When the children quarrel, I'm forming the habit of NOT telling them to say "I'm sorry" immediately. For me an immediate "I'm sorry" lacks truth. So instead, the offending child goes and spends some time away to think about how his or her actions or words might have hurt someone. When the child feels he or she has a handle on what has been done wrong, THEN the child may go and make amends. Sometimes it doesn't take long. Sometimes I'm needed to help guide thinking and understanding.

Confession is very situational, relational, and conversational. For these three reasons, it is a practice most effectively formed in children through intentional use of teachable moments and guided conversation throughout our everyday, walk-around lives.

Ways For You To Practice And Model Confession

Reflect: Where are you in your thoughts, attitudes, and practice of confession (telling the truth)?

Grace and forgiveness change how we treat ourselves, others, and our sin issues. What are your thoughts about this statement: "We need to see one another as saints who sin rather than as sinners who are saved"?

Respond: When we understand that all people, including those who have trusted Jesus as their Savior, are sinful creatures who God loves and continues to manage their sin with grace and mercy, our perspective changes. Write out some possible ways your perspective changed as you read this chapter.

Activities And Guided Conversations For Children

I Am You Are Forgiven

Use music to guide children to understand and practice confession and forgiveness. Here is a song that teaches the character virtue of forgiveness and the principles of confession discussed in this chapter.

I-M-U-R-F-O-R-G-I-V-E-N

(I Am, You Are Forgiven)

Lyrics and Music by Douglas C. Eltzroth [2]

One, two, three, four
I-M-U-R
F-O-R-G-I-V-E-N
I-M-I-M-F-O-R-G-I-V-E-N
I-M-I-M-F-O-R-G-I-V-E-N
I-M-I-M
That is why I sing and shout
That is why I dance about
I-M-I-M-F-O-R-G-I-V-E-N

I AGREED WITH God
That I'd done something wrong
I believed and He forgave
And gave to me this song

F-O-R-G-I-V-E-N
U-R-U-R-F-O-R-G-I-V-E-N
U-R-U-R-F-O-R-G-I-V-E-N
U-R-U-R

Now it's time to sing and shout
Now it's time to dance about
U-R-U-R-F-O-R-G-I-V-E-N

I confessed to God
That I'd done something wrong
I believed and He forgave
And gave to me this song
F-O-R-G-I-V-E-N
I-M-I-M-F-O-R-G-I-V-E-N
I-M-I-M-F-O-R-G-I-V-E-N
I-M-I-M

Learn and sing or say the words to "Forgiveness Song" (You may order a CD of the music by emailing your request to www.characterchoice.org.)

Talk About the Day

At mealtime, bed time, or show & tell time, make the suggestion to talk about the day.

Guided Conversation

"How was your day? What thoughts are in your mind that you have not been able to talk about? (Allow ideas.)

"I care about your mind. It is important not to hide thoughts, attitudes, or actions in your mind. What are some ways we could practice telling the truth? (Allow ideas.)

"We could take turns confessing the good things that happened today. Who would like to go first? (Allow children's ideas, but also model by saying something like, 'One of the best parts of my day has been _____.')

"Now we need to practice telling the truth, or confess, the thoughts, words, or actions that have been hurtful. Think about a time today when you might have hurt someone with your actions or your words. (Allow responses.)

"What are some ways to make this wrong right? (Pause.)

"Think about a time when you might have encouraged or helped someone with your actions or words. (Allow responses.)

"Telling the truth about hurtful and helpful thoughts, words, and actions is important in our life with God."

Confess Game

Prepare slips of paper with ideas or actions to be confessed. Some ideas might be "Jesus is Lord", "Oranges are orange", "Jesus will never leave you", "I hurt my friend _____ by _____", "I used an unacceptable word today", "The sky is blue", etc. Be sure to include some fun ideas. Place slips of paper in a container. Provide paper and pencils, pens, or colored markers for the children.

Guided Conversation

"We are learning about the practice of confession. To help us, we are going to play the "confess" game. The purpose of this game is to practice confessing what is true. I have written on slips of paper some ideas and actions to be confessed, and I have placed them in this container. First we can take turns drawing out the slips and reading the confession. You may add names and details as needed. (Children draw and read aloud the slips.)

"Now that we have drawn out and read all the slips of paper I have prepared, each of you may have a choice to prepare slips of paper. Print your idea or action on a slip of paper. Then place it in the container. Then we can have another round of drawings. (Children draw and read aloud the slips.)

"As we finish our game time, I have one more idea I would like to talk about. It seems that people do a lot of blaming. What are some times you have either been blamed for something or you blamed someone? (Allow responses.)

"Let's make it a habit to stop blaming. When blaming begins, let's chant: "No more blame! No more blame! No more blame!"

Two-Sided Coin

Provide a large, two-sided coin; cardboard circles for each child; glue, marking pens, and crayons; and printed words to be pasted on the circles.

Guided Conversation

"This art activity helps us think about and practice confession. Confession has two sides to it, something like this coin. (Pass coin to children.) What do you notice about this coin? (Allow responses.)

"On one side is one idea, and on the other side is another idea. The coin has two sides, but is one coin. Like the coin, confession has two sides, or parts, to it. One part is to tell the truth, or confess something that is true.

"Let's think about things that are true. Dogs have noses. Your turn. (Allow ideas.) Jesus is God's Son. Your turn. (Allow ideas.)

"Now the other side of confession is to agree with God that what you said, thought, or did is not what God wants. I'll start. I agree, Lord, I was really cranky with my daughter this morning. Your turn. (Allow ideas.)

"To help you remember the two sides of confession, I have materials for each of you to make a two-sided coin. On one side, paste the printed words 'To confess is to tell the truth.' On the other side, paste the words, 'To confess is to agree with God that what was said, thought, or done is not what God wants.'"

Chapter Ten

The Practice of Worship—Focus on God

You are worthy, our Lord and God, to receive glory and honor and power, for you created all things, and by your will they were created and have their being.

Revelation 4:11

Yet a time is coming and has now come when the true worshipers will worship the Father in spirit and truth, for they are the kind of worshipers the Father seeks.

John 4:23

After reading John 4:23 to a small group of children, a teacher remarked, "Worship is a direct order from God." Benjamin replied." Wow! God the Father is looking for worshipers!

If you were to explore Hebrew and Greek definitions of the word *worship*, you would discover that worship speaks of God's worth and our responsibility to adore Him. Usually we respond to this responsibility to worship God during the hours spent in a church worship service. But what about everyday worship in our everyday, walk-around lives? Is it possible that we are meant to integrate worship more fully into everyday life?

The Practice Of Worship For Followers Of Jesus

The intentional practice of worship as a discipline creates the opportunity to form a lifelong pattern and habit of a daily focus on God. This daily focus deepens our relationship with Him. "When we pour worship out over our daily lives, we grow ever more sensitive to God's voice and presence."[1] As our relationship with Him deepens, so does our desire to be with Him. "Worship does not satisfy our hunger for God—it whets our appetite. Our need for God is not taken care of by engaging in worship—it deepens."[2]

My child friendly wording for the spiritual discipline of *worship* is to focus on God. Worship is acknowledgement of who God is—His character, attitudes, and attributes. Worship is all about God.

> To *worship* is to focus on God.

In Scripture, worship is an attitude and action of thoughts and words directed to God that focus on who He is, why He exists, what He's done, how He thinks, why He came, and where He is. "The LORD is compassionate and gracious, slow to anger, abounding in love" (Psalm 103:8). "How many are your works, O LORD! In wisdom you made them all; the earth is full of your creatures. There is the sea, vast and spacious, teeming with creatures beyond number—living things both large and small" (Psalm 104: 24–25).

For us as followers of Jesus, worship is about God, keeping a right view of who God is, and keeping a view of God as the center of our worship. In Kathleen Chapman's book, *Teaching Kids Authentic Worship,* she challenges us to consider that God created worship for Himself alone.

Yes, we are to praise God! Yes, we are to thank Him for everything He has done for us. Yes, we are to ask Him about every part of our lives. But we must not confuse praising God with worshiping God. There is a difference. Praise is about *us*—our response to what God has done for *us*. Worship is about God—all adoration, adulation, awe, devotion, homage, honor, reverence, and wonder for who God is and what He has done. [3]

Teaching Tip

Remember that attitudes drive actions. Worship requires an attitude of giving "full attention moments" to God alone.

The spiritual discipline of worship requires a choice to purposefully focus on God coupled with honest desire. Worship also requires an attitude of giving "full attention moments" to God alone. Attitudes determine the quality of one's life in relationship to others because they require us to choose them. A positive attitude of worship is one that concentrates on God because we choose to obey His call to worship Him and because we want to worship Him.

The idea of worshiping "God alone" is a relatively new idea for me. In the past my worship thoughts have centered on praise and thanksgiving and probably a lot about me. It has been an eye opener for me to listen to and look at contemporary worship choruses. They are full of "I" adore You, "we" come before You, "I" need You, "I" am lost without You, "we" bow down before You—attitudes and ideas that are all about *us!* I am enjoying the choice to form new patterns and habits of worshiping "God alone."

Don't misunderstand me. Singing, praising, and giving thanks are ways to worship. But the challenge is to use these ways to focus on God. To think about who God is and what He does and then express those thoughts in ways that put the focus on Him—"You are strong. You are compassionate and loving. You are forgiving. You always tell the truth. You *are* integrity."

Focus On God's Character

Children may begin to know God and worship God at very early ages. Research shows that children learn the most and are most impressionable between birth and five years of age. Hours are spent forming attitudes, actions, and conduct. Children are taught to talk, walk, eat, read, count, dress themselves, and tie their shoes. They are taught to brush their teeth, wash their hands, and comb their hair. What occurs in these first formative years significantly affects them for life.

Compassion
Forgiveness
Integrity
Respect
Responsibility
Initiative
Cooperation
Perseverance

The next most valuable time is between the ages of five and eleven. In these years, children increase their level of comprehension, social interactions, cooperation, compassion, respect, and responsibility. During all of these early years (children ages birth–eleven), the focus of spiritual and character formation is to strengthen children's ability to reflect God's nature and character.

There is such a brief opportunity to impress children with God's character. These impressionable ages are a compelling reason to be deliberate and intentional about modeling and guiding children in beliefs, attitudes, and character habits and practices that reflect God's character. Guide children to be familiar with God's

Guide children to be familiar with God's character in order to worship Him. Becoming familiar with God by focusing on His character is in itself an act of worship.

character in order to worship Him. Becoming familiar with God by focusing on His character is in itself an act of worship.

Give children the character language to describe and worship God: God is a compassionate God. God loved us first. God is a forgiver. He made it possible for all people everywhere to be forgiven. God is a God of integrity. He is truth and always keeps His promises. Use a variety of words to describe God's character. Make it a pattern to saturate, soak, immerse, and engulf your children with God's character and personality!

Ideas For Worship Moments For You And For Your Children

Even though those of us who guide children may grasp the concept that worship is about God, our post-modern culture indoctrinates children to believe everything is about them. A true worship experience, one in which the focus is on God alone, may be the one place for children where the focus in their lives is completely off them. For this reason, the child friendly wording I use with children in tandem with the word worship is *focus on God*. "We are going to *worship God*. We are going to *focus on God*."

In our everyday, walk-around lives, it is important to develop and model our own patterns of private worship moments. These times may flow out of the weekly gathering of God's people. For example, later, when we are alone, we can sing the hymns or praise songs we sang with others. Our bodies may be used to powerfully affect our worship as well. As we sing to the Lord, we may expand on the bodily postures described in the hymns or songs. "Bow down" and "lift our hands" or positions that may not be comfortable in corporate worship like kneeling or lying prone on the floor may be more comfortably experienced in private.

Worship moments may happen anytime and anywhere. They may be spontaneous or planned. Think and say the word *worship,* and focus all thoughts, conversation, and adoration on God. Focus on His creation and attributes. Look at who He is, what He does, and why He came. Praise and thank Him with all that is within you. Whenever you do so, a worship moment is experienced.

> Worship moments may happen anytime and anywhere. They may be spontaneous or planned.

I wrote this chapter on April 14, and believe it or not, it was snowing where I live. I looked out my office window and saw God painting spring. It was a beautiful scene of a snow-covered stance of trees. The tops of the trees were covered with white, white snow. The branches were a deep, dark brown. Around the bottom of the trees were green tulip leaves, just pushing through the ground. It was a spontaneous worship moment for me.

A friend of mine described her structured worship moments.

As part of my morning practice of time spent with God, I follow a pattern of worship. It begins with a time of quiet, and then I say, "God, I'm here. Come and be with me." I then wait until there is a sense of God's presence. Intentionally I give praise statements to Him for each of these points, in this order. First, praise to Him for who He is, naming aspects of who He is that come to mind. Then praise to Him for His love, His power, and then His grace, again thinking of examples. Next, praise to Him for the things He has done most recently as they come to mind. Finally, praise to Him for the things He has done specifically in my life.

Worship moments happen when children are provided with opportunities to express their attitudes to and about God. The moment may be a verbal expression. It may be a facial expression without comment. It may be an expression of awe as a child touches a furry animal, examines the items in a bird's nest, smells a rose, listens to the sea roar in a shell, or tastes a juicy apple. Label these experiences as "worship moments."

In your church or community, children may learn to sing the doxology as a part of the worship experience. These words of the doxology are over two hundred years old, and yet they are still in common use during times of corporate worship: "Praise God from whom all blessings flow; Praise Him all creatures here below; praise him above, ye heavenly host: praise Father, Son and Holy Ghost." Think about times that you might sing the doxology in your classroom, home, when on a walk, in the car, and any time or place you want to praise God for His blessings.

Search for more worship songs. Begin this search by asking questions to direct a child's focus on God. "What tunes did God pick for birds to sing? What is the tune robins sing? Red-winged blackbirds? Meadowlarks?" (Use familiar birds in your area.)

Continue guiding the conversation by saying, "A worship song is one that talks about God, not us. It describes God, Jesus, or the Holy Spirit."

A worship song is one that talks about God, not us.

"Let's look in hymnals or songbooks and read the words in a few songs. Here is one example. 'He Is Lord; He is Lord; He is risen from the dead, and He is Lord. Ev-'ry knee shall bow, ev'ry tongue confess that Jesus Christ is Lord.'[4]"

Here is a list of worship songs from Kathleen Chapman's book, *Teaching Authentic Worship.*[5]

"Our God Is an Awesome God"
"Holy God, Most Holy God"

"A Might Fortress"
"Crown Him with Many Crowns"
"You Are Lord"
"Jesus, Name Above All Names"
"To Every Generation"
"You Are Crowned with Many Crowns"
"He Reigns"
"King of Kings"
"Celebrate Jesus"
"Blessed Be the Name of the Lord"
"Jesus, What a Friend of Sinners"
"Holy, Holy, Holy!"
"To God Be the Glory"

Take children outside on a beautiful day. Read or say Psalm 66:5 (NLT), "Come and see what our God has done, what awesome miracles he performs for people!" Encourage children to raise their hands to God. Say, "Now is the time to worship." Watch and see how children choose to use their bodies to worship God. They may choose to sing, dance, or jump. Talk about some of the flowers and trees you see. Talk about the texture and color of the bark, about the different colors, sizes, and shapes of trees and flowers.

Take children on a walk and have them find one "piece" of God's creation. Then if weather and environment permit, have children share why they think God created what they chose. Be prepared to read Bible verses mentioning various items of creation.

Branch (or vine) – John 15:4
Dirt (or dust) – Psalm 18:42
Flower – 1 Kings 6:29
Leaves – Mark 11:13
Water or vegetables – Daniel 1:12
Wood – Genesis 6:14
Worm – Isaiah 51:8

One last idea to model and guide children to create personal names for God. In a book called *Tales of the Not Forgotten* is a name for God that is new to me: Storyweaver. The name Storyweaver is used throughout the book to demonstrate how God "weaves" our stories and lives into the stories and lives of others to accomplish His purposes for all of us. Each of us may create our personal names for God (such as Storyweaver) based on how we see or experience Him at work in our lives and the lives of others. One person I know created her personal name for God after a dramatic experience of rescue in her life. The name "Just-in-Time God" has proven itself true many times in her life since then.

Ways For You To Practice And Model Worship

Come, let us bow down in worship, let us kneel before the LORD our Maker; for he is our God and we are the people of his pasture, the flock under his care. Psalm 95:6–7

These verses call us to worship with others who believe in God, the Lord, who is our Maker. We come together as God's flock, not as individuals. The gathering together of a community of followers of Christ to worship has been a practice since the time of early Christianity.

In contrast to the religions of the East, the Christian faith has strongly emphasized corporate worship. Even under highly dangerous circumstances the early community was urged not to forsake the assembling of themselves together (Heb. 10:25). The Epistles speak frequently of the believing community as the "body of Christ." As human life is unthinkable without head, arms, and legs, so it was unthinkable for those Christians to live in isolation from one another.[6]

When more than one or two come into public worship with the intentional purpose to focus on God alone, it can change the atmosphere of a room. Here is a practical, intentional way to accomplish the idea of changing the atmosphere to be a focus on God.

Live throughout your week in individual worship, daily giving full attention moments to God. Since you have focused on God and worshiped God throughout the week, you know you are able to focus on God when you gather for public worship.

> Live throughout your week in individual worship, daily giving full attention moments to God.

Plan to enter the service ten minutes before the service begins. Instead of visiting with the people next to you, begin to focus on the King of Glory. Think on God's majesty, glory, and compassionate tenderness as revealed in Jesus. Picture what Isaiah described of the Lord, "high and lifted up," and the seraphs calling to one another, "Holy, holy, holy is the LORD Almighty" (Isaiah 6:3). Invite the Holy Spirit's presence to be manifest.

Then begin to lift into the light of Christ the worship leaders and pastors. Picture the spirit of God surrounding them and the power of the Lord to be in them so that they may speak the truth boldly. As people enter the service, be aware of some who need to be lifted into the hope and refreshment of God's presence. Ask the Spirit of God to give them courage and wisdom for the circumstances present in their lives.

When only a few in any congregation make these practices a habit, the worship experience of all is deepened.

Reflect: The practice of worship as a discipline creates the opportunity to form patterns of daily focus on God. When and where in your everyday, walk-around life do you focus on God?

Respond: Have you tried the idea of writing a letter to God? If not, try now. Write only about God. Write everything wonderful about *Him*. You are not to mention yourself. No first person pronouns (I, me, we, us). Fill the letter with words that adore God.

Make it a lifelong practice and a habit to focus on God. Think about who God is and what He does, and then express these thoughts daily by giving "full attention moments" to God.

Activities And Guided Conversations For Children

You must know someone in order to worship that person. Children know Justin Bieber, the Jonas Brothers, Miley Cyrus, and other famous people they see on television. Arguably, in some ways they worship these people. It is important to guide children to know God by thinking about, exploring, imagining, and experiencing God so they can worship God with understanding, enthusiasm, and excited anticipation. *Knowing* and *experiencing* God makes it possible to truly *worship* God. Model worship as you guide children with some of these ideas.

Write a Letter

Provide paper, pencils, pens, markers, and crayons. Encourage children to write a letter to God and write only about God.

Guided Conversation

"We are practicing worship. Worship is to focus on God. Let's try worshiping God by writing a letter to Him. Write everything wonderful about Him. You are not to mention yourself. No personal pronouns (I, me, we, us). Fill the letter with words that adore God."

As children finish their letters, invite them to share what they have written. (You may discover that their first attempt results in words like "Dear God, I love you, thank you for my family and friends. Thank you for my dog, Benji …" So continue to increase their understanding of worshiping only God by saying:

Telling God how much *you* love Him and thanking Him for people and events in *your* life is wonderful, but it is about *you*, *your* love, *your* family, *your* friends. The idea is for you to focus *on God* and write only *about God*. Be patient. It may take some practice. Listen to this example and then try again. (Read the letter that follows out loud.)

Dear God,

You made the stars and the sky. You love SOOOO big, and you don't get mad easy. You made cats, dogs, parrots, and people.

Love, Sarah P., age 7[7]

God's Names

Learn the names of God. We tend to underestimate what children are able to learn and understand. For younger children, choose the simple names. Preschool age children understand to different degrees the word and concept of love. For older children provide a copy of the list of names for God.

Guided Conversation

For younger children

"How would you explain the meaning of the word *love* to someone in your family or a friend? (Allow responses.) We are learning ways to worship to focus on God. One way is to say His name. God has many names. Listen to these Bible words. 'God is love' (1 John 4:8). What name do these Bible words use for a name for God? (Allow response.) Then say, 'Another name for God is Love'."

NOTE: It is helpful for younger children to begin with familiar and concrete ideas. You might move on from "Love" to "Abba" and explain that Abba means "Daddy".

For older children

"As we practice moments of worship, moments to focus on God, let's think about other names for God. Here is a list of some of the many names for God. Some of the names listed also have the meaning of the name. As you read through the list, circle two that you would like to use now and for the next week as you worship—focus on God. (Pause to allow time to accomplish the task.)

- **Abba** (Romans 8:15) means "Daddy" (the name that is a firsthand experience for children).
- **Alpha and Omega** (Revelation 22:13). *Alpha* means the beginning and *Omega* means the end. Talk with children about how God was here before anything else or anyone else. Watch their attention grow as they ask, "Was God here before cars and planes?" "Was God here before computers and TV?" "Was God here before Grandma and Grandpa?"
- **Ancient of Days** (Daniel 7:9)
- **Christ, Son of the living God** (Matthew 16:16)
- **Counselor** (Isaiah 9:6)
- **Creator** (1 Peter 4:19)
- **Emmanuel means "God with us"** (Matthew 1:23)
- **Eternal God** (Deut. 33:27)
- **Everlasting Father** (Isaiah 9:6)
- **The Everlasting God** (Isaiah 40:28–31)
- **Father** (Matthew 6:9)
- **Great Shepherd** (Hebrews 13:20)
- **Holy Spirit** (John 15:26)
- **I Am** (Exodus 3:14, John 8:58)
- **Jesus** (Matthew 1:21)
- **King of Kings** (1 Timothy 6:15)
- **Lamb of God** (John 1:29)
- **Lord** (John 13:13)
- **Love** (1 John 4:8)
- **Messiah** (John 4:25)
- **Mighty God** (Isaiah 9:6)
- **Prince of Peace (Isaiah 9:6)**
- **Redeemer (Job 19:25)**
- **Savior (Luke 2:11)**
- **Spirit of God (Genesis 1:2)**
- **Teacher (John 13:13)**
- **Wonderful Counselor (Isaiah 9:6)**

(Different translations and versions of the Bible may use different words than those listed here, which are taken from the NIV ©1984. You may wish to consult the versions you use and build a list of your own.)

"Now it is time to worship—focus on God. Say a name you have chosen and add any words you wish. Listen to others as they speak their choice of name for God. Let us begin. Who would like to start?" (If needed lead in an example.)

NOTE: The song *Jesus, You Are Holy*[8] offers numerous names to sing worship with a focus on God.

Another way to learn the names of God and practice worship, focus on God, is to say (or sing) this song.

Holy, holy; Jesus, You are holy;
Lord Almighty; Jesus, You are Lord.
You are Lord of Lords.
You are King of Kings.
Living bread from heaven, the Faithful and True.
You're the Lamb of God, slain before the world;
We surrender all that we are to You.
You are the Way; You are the Truth; You are the Life; and life You give.
In You is life; In You is love; In You is hope; In You we live.

Make it a practice to use the many names of God in teachable moments and your everyday, walk-around life to increase children's familiarity with God's character and attributes.

God's Presence

Lead children in this practice of affirming God's presence 24/7.

Guided Conversation

"Here is a way to worship, focus on God, and be aware of His presence with us. Clasp your hands together, place your hands in front of your body, and say, 'God before me.'

"Now place your hands to your side and say, 'God beside me.'

"Now place your hands behind you and say, 'God behind me.'

"Place your hands on your feet and say, 'God below me.'

"Raise your hands over your head and say, 'God above me.'"

Repeat motions and say: "Christ before me, Christ beside me, Christ behind me, Christ below me, Christ above me."

Repeat motions and say: "Holy Spirit before me, Holy Spirit beside me, Holy Spirit behind me, Holy Spirit below me, Holy Spirit above me. Amen."

Chapter Eleven

The Practice of Guidance—Search for God's Presence and Direction

For this God is our God forever and ever; he will be our guide even to the end.

> Psalm 48:14

Make plans by seeking advice.

> Proverbs 20:18

Whether you turn to the right or to the left, your ears will hear a voice behind you, saying, "This is the way; walk in it."

> Isaiah 30:21

"Who is God, and what is He like?"

"How is Jesus different than God?"

"How is Jesus like God?"

"Why do people do bad things?"

Children ask wonderful questions!

We, like children, search for God. We want to know what He is like. We want to be aware of His presence and direction for our lives. Each morning I try to have a time with God, praising Him and thanking Him for the events and people I have encountered the day before. I jot down a list of tasks for the day. Then I ask God to order the day. It brings me joy each morning to review how the previous day went in relationship to the tasks I listed and what was accomplished or redirected. This life-long pattern and habit gives me evidence of God's presence, guidance, and direction. What ways have you found to seek and find God's presence and direction?

The Practice Of Guidance For Followers Of Jesus

My child friendly wording for the spiritual discipline of *guidance* is to "search for and discern God's presence and direction." This practice is accomplished individually as well as with the help of trusted followers of Christ. The discipline of guidance enables us to fall in line with God's purposes moment by moment.

The spiritual discipline of *guidance* is to search for and discern God's presence and direction.

During the years when I lived as a single person, I had a strong desire and very real need to seek God's guidance. The strength of this desire resulted in precious growth in the quality of attentiveness to God. Over time it developed in me an intuitive sense of God's presence (or my lack of attentiveness) in any given moment. The practice of the discipline of guidance has enabled me to discover and discern God's direction more clearly, and it has given me confidence in large and small decisions.

God's guidance for me occurs often in the everyday maintenance issues of life: to locate a certain passage in a book I have recently read, to phone a friend who has just been diagnosed with a frightening illness, to be aware of my grandchildren's desire to interact with me about their lives, and to be reminded to lift loved ones into the presence of the Holy One for encouragement and guidance.

Seeking to clearly discern God's guidance develops a familiarity with God's voice—the tone, inflection, and content—just as we become familiar with the voice of a loved one or friend we know well. Through the regular, intentional practice of guidance, we become able to struggle with and understand answers to many of our questions about God. Who is God in this moment for me? What is God doing in my life? Where is God at work, and how can I join Him? How can I be most genuine in response to His guidance? Ruth Haley Barton describes this kind of discernment as "a way of looking at all of life with a view to sensing the movement of God's Spirit and abandoning ourselves to it just as we might give ourselves to the experience of floating down a river."[1]

Practice seeking God's presence, guidance, and direction in the mundane things of your life. When you are searching for the keys to your car or the glasses you have laid down, ask God to help you find what is misplaced or lost. Stop searching for the item, remind yourself that God is present, and listen for His guidance. It saves a lot of time! The older I become, the more I rely on this kind of guidance.

Practice moments of gratitude to enable you to perceive God more clearly. Rehearse the ways and times God has blessed your life, family, and friends. Rejoice in your intimate love relationship with God the Father, Jesus the Son, and the Holy Spirit. Whenever you sense anxiousness, remind yourself that your security and guidance rest in God and He is totally trustworthy.

By now, as you have been exploring and learning the spiritual disciplines covered so far in this book, you likely have discovered that approaches to practicing them often overlap. Recently as I have needed to make some lifetime decisions, I have found myself using a *breath prayer* in the practice of guidance. A breath prayer is like this. Breathe in and say (think), "Abba," or a favorite name for God. Then breathe out and say (think), "Please give direction." Breathe in and say (think), "Breath of Life" or a favorite name for God. Then breathe out and say (think), "Please give discernment."

Another example of the overlap in the practice of guidance is the use of Scripture readings (Chapter 1: Meditation) and solitude (Chapter 6: Solitude) for the purpose of listening to God's voice and seeking His guidance. When you ask the Holy Spirit to guide you moment by moment, He comes close to you, and you are able to sense Him.

Practice Guidance With Trusted Followers Of Christ

Guidance is not always an individual discipline. "Make plans by seeking advice," says King Solomon in Proverbs 20:18. There is great benefit for each of us to identify people with whom we can process decisions. The advice of trusted followers of Christ can confirm and sometimes augment the direction we are hearing from God.

Explore your relationships in your family and your community. Who do you trust? Why do you trust them? What do you see in their life with God? Do they desire a way of life that creates space for God's transforming work and guidance?

Examine your attitude of isolation. Often we hide our true thoughts and attitudes from others. We may fear that our true thoughts and attitudes may not be accepted. Or perhaps we fear that we may not be able to accept the thoughts and attitudes of others. The discipline of guidance requires practice with others in much the same way teams (sport, missionary, business) come together to function and grow in maturity.

> The discipline of guidance requires practice with others in much the same way teams come together to function and grow in maturity.

Make a choice to invite others to offer you guidance, especially if you have avoided the idea of seeking help when faced with difficult decisions. Consider becoming part of a small group whose purpose for meeting is to pray; to encourage one another; to hold each other accountable for personal spiritual growth; and to focus on what God has done, is doing, and will do in members' lives as they practice the spiritual disciplines.

Focus On God's Character

Foundation Virtues:
Compassion
Forgiveness
Integrity
Respect
Responsibility
Initiative
Cooperation
Perseverance

Family Virtues:
Discernment

Becoming people who reflect God's character requires that we and the children we serve desire and intentionally practice living in an intimate relationship with God. Or in other words, we enjoy life with God. In our waking and in our sleeping, in our thinking and saying, in being and doing, in our everyday, walk-around life, we are with God.

God is committed to our character, not to our comfort. He allows trials to form our spirit. "The testing of your faith develops perseverance. Perseverance

> God is committed to our character, not to our comfort.

must finish its work so that you may be mature and complete, not lacking anything" (James 1:3–4). The character virtues of perseverance, initiative, and discernment are enhanced in the practice of guidance.

Perseverance is continual, steady effort made to fulfill some purpose, goal, task, or commitment. It means persistence in spite of difficulties, opposition, or discouragement. Perseverance is the refusal to give up when things are difficult. It is the habit of following through and finishing what was started.

Encourage children to persevere in the practice of guidance. Give them examples from the Bible of people who persevered in following God even when life was difficult. The account of Joseph in Genesis 37–39 is a great example of ways that God guides and a great example of Joseph's trust and perseverance.

The virtue of initiative is choosing to take the first step in thinking, doing, or learning. It includes being responsible for follow-through. Initiative involves demonstrating responsible thoughts and actions without being prompted or without being influenced by limited choices. The following story demonstrates a child's initiative that was not influenced by a teacher's limited choice.

A church leader in a small inner city church explained a mission's project in India to six elementary children in this way:

With just three quarters, each of you may sponsor a child in India who has never heard the name of Jesus to attend a week of Vacation Bible School. If each of you brings just three quarters next Sunday, our class will make it possible for six children to learn about Jesus.

The following Sunday, when the quarters were to be collected, the teacher was surprised to see 7-year-old Cameron carrying a large, heavy bag into the room. "Look, Miss Roberts! Here are my quarters," the child exclaimed with a radiant smile.

"Oh, Cameron," she said. "You only needed to bring three quarters."

"I know you said that," replied Cameron, "but I wanted to sponsor as many children as I could, not just one. So I put all of the quarters I had at home in a bag, and then I asked everyone in my family and all of the neighbors on my street if they would give me quarters too."

"Here," he said, handing her the bag. "How many children may I sponsor?"

Encourage children to take the initiative to ask for guidance. Label attitudes and actions when you observe children seeking to discover and discern God's direction for their lives. "Stefanie, I see your attitude to desire to ask God to help you decide on your summer activities. Your action demonstrates initiative."

Learning and practicing discernment, which is a *family virtue* of integrity, enhances the practice of guidance. To discern means to clearly observe the difference between one concept or idea and another. Learning to discern helps us in our search for God's presence and direction.

Ideas For Children To Practice Guidance

Children are often adept at sensing God's presence and knowing when God is giving them guidance. Listen to and affirm what children have discerned about God's presence and direction.

Keep in mind that words have tremendous power. Words are able to create and build relationships, knowledge, attitudes, and understanding. The words we use and the way we guide conversation greatly impact spiritual and character formation in children, their families, and communities.

In order to offer children a fuller experience of life with God, it is our responsibility to draw out, in everyday, walk-around experiences, an understanding of God and God's desires for the people He created.

Help children wrestle with difficult issues and learn good decision-making skills. For example, a child says, "I can't make friends." You respond, "It is hard to try something when you're not sure you can do it. Who would you like to

In order to offer children a fuller experience of life with God, it is our responsibility to draw out, in everyday, walk-around experiences, an understanding of God and God's desires for the people He created.

become your friend? (Allow and accept an answer). Then offer some concrete help. "What books or games does _____ like?" Depending on the child's response, guide the child to ask the identified friend what he or she likes to eat, or what is a favorite game. Then discuss how the friend might be invited to be with the child and enjoy these activities together. Be sure to invite the child to ask God to help guide and discern this adventure.

An important pattern to live and model the discipline of guidance is to encourage children to ask questions and then do your best to answer. Label your desire to help them find God's guidance: "Thank you, Lisa, for your questions. I may not know all the answers, but I want to help you as you search for God's guidance." Direct them to ask their questions to other trusted adults as well—parents, grandparents, aunts, uncles, coaches, and teachers.

Children's questions cover many areas and range from simple to complex. Have courage to enter into these kinds of conversations that promote critical thinking. A broad definition of *critical thinking* is the disciplined practice of thinking, imagining, formulating, and testing for the truth. Here are some children's questions that promote critical thinking.

- Why are certain attitudes and actions important?

- What makes an attitude or action right or wrong?

- Why are some prayers answered and not others?

- Who is God, and what is He like?

- How is Jesus different than God?

- How is Jesus like God?

- Why do people do bad things?

- Why do some friends and family members not follow Jesus?

- Why do some people who follow Jesus have "attitude attacks" or make destructive choices?

- Why is church important?

- Why did Jesus have to die?

- Why is it important to go to Sunday school and church?

- Why doesn't God just do stuff without us having to pray?

Teaching Tip:

Promote critical thinking. A broad definition of *critical thinking* is the disciplined practice of thinking, imagining, formulating, and testing for the truth.

Guide children with real-life examples and examples from the Bible in order to build their trust of the Bible, God, and others. Listen and discover what your children think. Cultivate a nonjudgmental, unconditional, loving attitude as you guide and explore their important questions.

Choose one of the questions listed in this chapter to focus on and practice with the children you serve. Begin with one that fits your lifestyle and seems comfortable to you. For instance, when there is a conflict about an attitude or action such as choosing to spend time with an individual, ask the question, "What makes an attitude or action right or wrong?" Continue with the question, "Why is it important to discern certain attitudes and actions when choosing to spend time with a person?" Remember, your purpose is to be able to hear and discover what children think to enable both you and the children to improve in the ability to discern God's presence, guidance, and direction for your lives.

Ways For You To Practice And Model Guidance

Reflect: The practice of guidance as a discipline creates the opportunity to improve our ability to discern God's presence and direction for our lives. The practice may include reading Scripture, listening to God's voice in solitude, and seeking counsel from others who are wise and trustworthy.

Where in your life are you making space for Scripture reading and solitude? Where in your life are you seeking guidance from others whose purpose is to encourage one another? In what relationships do you hold each other accountable for personal and spiritual growth, prayer, and focus on what God has done and is doing and will do in your lives as you practice the spiritual disciplines?

Respond: Consider keeping a one-week record of all the times you are aware
                    of being guided by God through your Scripture reading, other peo-
                    ple, planned or unplanned incidences or interactions, literature,
                    movies, and artwork. At the end of the week, look over your re-
                    cord. What have you discovered? How much space did you make for
                    Scripture reading and solitude? Has your schedule kept you from
                    hearing God speaking? Have you been open to hearing God's voice
                    in ways you don't expect, or are you limiting Him by missing other
                    ways by which you might hear His voice?

                    Examine your life in relation to those who you search out for guid-
                    ance. Look at your community. Make a list of your good friends, and
                    note next to their names why they are good friends. Who else is in
                    your life to offer guidance and significant help? Write their names
                    down and why you would receive their guidance and significant help.

Activities And Guided Conversation For Children

Discernment Game

This game of discernment is a fun activity for groups of three or five. Provide small paper cups filled with enough peanuts (be aware of allergies) or raisins to give each player four. Either make a copy of the Game Directions found at the end of this chapter or post them on a PowerPoint, chalkboard, or poster so that children may see the instructions as they play the game.

Guided Conversation

"Learning to discern helps us in our search for God's presence and direction. To discern means to clearly observe the difference between one concept or idea and another. The game we are about to play is a discernment game. This is how the game is played.

"First, make groups (circles) of three but no more than five people. (Allow time for children to form their groups.)

"Now I am giving one cup of peanuts (or raisins) to each group (circle). Please listen to the instructions. Each player holds four peanuts or raisins in one hand, mak-ing a fist with the other hand. (Pause.) In each group (circle), choose one player to be the first counter. (Pause.) As the counter counts, all players pat their fists on their knees three times. On the third pat of your fists, each player extends 0–5 fingers. The counter then counts the total fingers showing in your group. The counter then follows the directions on the Game Directions sheet for the total count of your group.

"Continue to repeat with different players taking a turn to be the counter. Play until time is called or one person does not have any peanuts (or raisins) left. Then together we will have a time to talk about what you *discern*. Any questions? Okay, go!"

When the game is finished, ask these questions:

1. Was it more fun to give or to receive?
2. What was your attitude when taking a person's last piece?
3. What was your attitude when you gave away your last piece?
4. What if you were playing with M&M'S® instead of peanuts (or raisins)?

Game Directions

| **0-1** | Give a piece to the person on your right. |

| **2-3** | Give a piece to the youngest person. |

| **4-5** | Give a piece to the person on your left. |

| **6-7** | Give a piece to anyone you choose. |

| **8-9** | Ask the person on your left to give a piece to the person on your right. |

| **10-11** | Don't give a piece away. |

| **12-13** | Eat one piece. |

| **14-15** | Choose one person to eat one piece. |

Chapter Twelve

The Practice of Celebration—Have Joy and Delight

If you obey my commands, you will remain in my love, just as I have obeyed my Father's commands and remain in his love. I have told you this so that my joy may be in you and that your joy may be complete.

John 15:10–11

Celebration is utter delight and joy in ourselves, our life, and our world as a result of our faith and confidence in God's greatness, beauty, and goodness.

The RENOVARÉ *Spiritual Formation Bible*[1]

On just an ordinary day, a child remarked, "Let's make today a special day, Mommy."

Celebration is the center of all practice of the spiritual disciplines. In this life with God, the inner part of the way of Jesus includes His desire to have His joy be in us. In John 15:10–11, Jesus gives us the way to His joy by connecting joy to obedience. In our life with God, then, obedience becomes that which produces genuine joy.

Most children are capable of expressing joy naturally and often. What they need is people who help them name that joy that comes from God and provide ways to experience and express it. Recently I was on a shuttle bus and had the opportunity to observe a three- or four-year-old child using a box for a guitar. She was strumming and singing some made-up words to a familiar tune. As I caught her eye, she giggled with joy. Our non-verbal conversation across the aisle was filled with smiles, giggles, and joy. The little girl's mother consistently gave her boundaries, reminding her about the tone of her voice and the need to remain in her seat. The logical consequence of the child's obedience was joy in a difficult environment.

For children, obedience is often perceived as something difficult or imposed on them. When we are able to connect acts and attitudes of obedience to children's natural joy, then obedience becomes a source of joy and delight. My child friendly wording for *celebration* is "having joy and delight."

> The spiritual discipline of *celebration* is having joy and delight.

Children have the capacity to see and experience celebration in joyful and delightful ways. Having joy and delight in the present moment, they are less hampered by the past or worried about the future.

The Practice of Celebration for Followers of Jesus

The spiritual discipline of celebration for followers of Jesus is a way of thinking about life. In this way of thinking, everything may be encircled with an attitude of gratefulness for events that are a part of each day.

Whether you are a person inclined to be positive or negative, the intentional practice of the spiritual discipline of celebration enhances gratefulness and joy. Joy is not dependent on circumstances. True joy is a by-product of obedient living in God's presence.

Linking joy with obedience may be a new thought for you, as it has been for many others. Valerie Hess expresses her experience:

> When I first came across the concept that obedience equals joy, I thought, *No way! That makes no sense.* But because it bothered me, the words stuck in my mind. And then one day on my regular exercise walk, the puzzle pieces came together. That morning, I observed two different dogs and their owners. In the first case, the dog was well trained. It was off-leash but clearly under voice command. Therefore, the owner could trust it to run a bit, which it was delighting in doing. This dog's tail was wagging enthusiastically, and it was obviously relishing the many smells of the mountain meadow.

The second dog was not well trained. In fact, as its owner yelled futilely for it to come, it dashed pell-mell across a very busy street without even slowing down. The owner ran breathlessly after it, and I eventually lost sight of them. That dog could have been badly hurt—or worse. And while it may have looked as if it were enjoying itself, we all know how it would have felt had it been struck by some unsuspecting driver.[2]

As obedience to God's ways becomes the ordinary attitude and response in our daily lives, the result is a "completed joy" (John 15:11) and the ability to experience genuine celebration. Without obedience to live our lives as God intends, attempts at celebrating become empty and hollow. Yes, people may find temporary joy at a concert or even celebrating at a church service and hope that somehow the infusion of joy will carry them through the day or week. The hope is that something will change the maintenance or misery of their daily lives and give them genuine and complete joy. But God desires to do a transforming work in the lives of followers of Jesus, which leads them to His genuine and complete joy. His desire is to *transform* the maintenance and misery of life, not bypass it.

> Joy is not found in singing a particular kind of music or in getting with the right kind of group or even in exercising the charismatic gifts of the Spirit, good as all these may be. Joy is found in obedience. When the power that is in Jesus reaches into our work and play and redeems them, there will be joy where once there was mourning. To overlook this is to miss the meaning of the Incarnation.[3]

All of the disciplines include acts and attitudes of obedience, and as a result, celebration is at the center of all practice of the spiritual disciplines. The end result of the practice of the spiritual disciplines in our everyday, walk-around lives is the Spirit of God's transformation of our lives. As we experience God's transformation, we know and experience His genuine joy.

All of the disciplines include acts and attitudes of obedience, and as a result, celebration is at the center of all practice of the spiritual disciplines.

Celebration Brings Strength

The practice of celebration builds the attitudes, emotions, and actions of joy into our lives. And joy makes us strong. "The joy of the LORD is your strength" (Nehemiah 8:10). The strength of joy is needed as we go through the challenges of life.

In the movie, "Steel Magnolias," is a scene where the mother who has just buried her daughter is weeping and screaming and yelling out her anger and grief to a group of her friends. She says something like, "I am so angry, I just can't do this! I'm supposed to die first. I have always been ready to die first. I just want to hit someone!" One of the women pushes another woman forward and says, "Here, hit Louisa." Louisa responds, "What? Are you crazy? Why hit me?" They all dissolve into peals of laughter. The laughter and joy over Louisa's response releases the grief and tension of the moment.

Likewise, the hope of joy and the strength that results from joy carry us through difficult years of change, adjustments, and grief. Mothers endure childbirth because of the hope of the joy of that precious new baby. Children begin sport activities or begin to play an instrument of choice, but they do not keep at it for long unless they experience the joy of their choice. Parents stay steady through teen years and choose joy in the adventure of their teens becoming responsible adults. The joy is what sustains all beginnings.

The practice of celebration makes possible the continuation and consistency of the practice of all the spiritual disciplines. Without joyous celebration being poured into the practice of the disciplines, we will sooner or later stray from their practice. Joy gives us energy and makes us strong to persevere.

> The practice of celebration makes possible the continuation and consistency of the practice of all the spiritual disciplines.

Celebration Brings Security

A sense of security and indifference to things begins when we begin to trust God for everything. As we increasingly trust the Lord for everything, we have a growing sense of security and more indifference to things that do not last. The apostle Paul tells us, "Rejoice in the Lord always. I will say it again: Rejoice!" Then he tells us how to do this: "Do not be anxious about anything, but in everything, by prayer and petition, with thanksgiving, present your requests to God." The result is "the peace of God, which transcends all understanding, will guard your hearts and your minds in Christ Jesus" (Philippians 4:4, 6, 7).

Jesus offers us this same sense of security when He says, "Do not worry about your life, what you will eat or drink; or about your body, what you will wear" (Matthew 6:25).

Followers of Christ are called to be secure and free of care. But our culture trains us to be consumers, to fill our lives with things and find our security in possessions. In contrast, the Bible trains us to be secure in trusting God to give us wisdom and an indifference to things. The spirit of celebration will be in us when we learn to "not be anxious about anything."

But what about the hard times of life? Philippians 4:8 encourages us to think about "whatever is true, whatever is noble, whatever is right, whatever is pure, whatever is lovely, whatever is admirable—if anything is excellent or praiseworthy." This is God's way to joy. When we fill our minds and lives with simple, good things and consistently give God thanks for them, the result is a joy-filled life, even in the midst of hard times. The choice to think on these things and form attitudes of trust in Christ are acts of the will. These acts of the will require intention and effort. That is why celebration is a discipline. Joy is the result of consciously choosing how to think and live.

> Joy is the result of consciously choosing how to think and live.

More Benefits Of Celebration

Another important benefit of celebration is that it keeps us from taking our circumstances and ourselves too seriously. We can become weary with well doing, even in serving God and others, just as our bodies become weary from overwork. Patterns of celebration give us the opportunity to relax and enjoy good friends, good conversation, and people who love God and love life.

> It is an occupational hazard of devout folk to become stuffy bores. This should not be. Of all people, we should be the most free, alive, interesting. Celebration adds a note of gaiety, festivity, hilarity to our lives.[4]

Before our marriage, my husband and I were very weary from wedding preparations and combining two households, our families, and work responsibilities. So I suggested that we invite one of our favorite couples to have dinner at my house. Instead they responded with the invitation to have dinner at their house. As we drove to their home, we remarked on how great it was to just be going to a place where we would have no responsibility and could relax and share each other's lives. We left refreshed, filled with good food, and joy in our shared love of God and life. It was a time of celebration in the midst of our circumstances. Celebration may also be an effective antidote for times of sadness or grief. God identifies with our grief and sadness. He desires and has the ability to draw us from the deepest pit.

> "Celebration is not only a part of special occasions, but an ongoing awareness that every moment is special and asks to be lifted up and recognized as a blessing from on high."
>
> *Henri Nouwen*

Depression is an epidemic today, and the practice of the discipline of celebration by making a conscious choice to think on what is good, play a game, or dance to some favorite tunes is one way to release the sense of sadness. Celebration moves people out of grief and sadness into knowing that life is still good.

A recent startling statistic was noted in the February 2011 *Children's Ministry Magazine*. The source of the information was Uplift Program. "Preschoolers are the fastest-growing group for antidepressants. At least 4% of preschoolers—over a million—are clinically depressed."[5] It would seem that these children, their families, and caretakers of young children would benefit from the practice of celebration.

One other benefit of the practice of celebration is to give us perspective. The practice of this discipline is not done to manufacture happiness. The practice makes it possible to surround everything we are and do with celebration. Forming lifelong attitudes, patterns, and habits of celebration encourages us to have an awareness of the bigger picture of our lives and the God-given gifts that are a part of our life with God.

The attitude of celebration makes possible the celebration not only of holidays, birthdays, weddings, and other special events, but also the coming of spring after a hard winter, a child skipping down a walk, and the splendor of an ocean or mountain range. Instead of moaning about going to work, we are thankful for a job, thankful for a courteous person holding a door open, hot running water, or a kind word from a flight attendant. Celebration enhances the awareness that every gift is from God and is a reason to celebrate the reality and reliability of life with God.

> Celebration enhances the awareness that every gift is from God and is a reason to celebrate the reality and reliability of life with God.

Celebration often, in both the simple and special aspects of life, develops the attitude of gratefulness. This attitude of gratefulness drives the action of having eyes and ears open to the consistent and present activity of God.

Focus On God's Character

Compassion
Forgiveness
Integrity
Respect
Responsibility
Initiative
Cooperation
Perseverance

Character is who we are expressed in action—in how we live and in what we do. Our lifelong challenge is to take on God's character of compassion, forgiveness, integrity, respect, responsibility, initiative, cooperation, and perseverance. As you think of celebration activities, identify and label character virtues connected to them.

> Character is who we are expressed in action — in how we live, and in what we do.

To guide children in the virtue of compassion, talk about different situations in which someone seems left out. Encourage children to notice a child at school who seems left out and to reach out to help him or her to be included. For example, a child may sit by a new student to help him be included. Ask the question, "What other way could you be compassionate and help a new person at school?" Celebrate the joy of being a compassionate person.

To guide children in the virtue of forgiveness, when there is conflict in a classroom or at home, talk about how the conflict might be resolved. Ask who needs to forgive and who needs to be forgiven. Talk about the joy that is experienced when you forgive someone. Talk about the joy you have when you are forgiven. Celebrate the joy of forgiveness.

To guide children in the virtue of integrity, have a conversation with children about their language. Challenge them with the following to practice three ways to be people of integrity who are truthful about their speech:

Before you speak, ask yourself:

1. Is it true?
2. Is it kind?
3. Is it necessary?

If not, let it go unsaid.

Celebrate the joy and freedom experienced by being truthful and acting with integrity. Label their practice by saying, "You are becoming a person of integrity." You may also tie the practice of integrity to John 8:32, "The truth will set you free."

Use your creative imagination with godly virtues to model, label, and celebrate becoming a person who reflects God's character.

Ideas For Children To Practice Celebration

Most of us find it easy to celebrate birthdays, anniversaries, holidays, and other happy events we experience. The challenge is to learn new patterns to practice celebration every day. That takes discipline.

Think about what you enjoy in life. "We engage in celebration when we enjoy ourselves, our life, our world, *in conjunction with* our faith and confidence in God's greatness, beauty, and goodness. We concentrate on *our* life and world as God's work and as God's gift to us."[6] What do you enjoy—singing, dancing, shouting, sport events, laughter, play, and opportunities to accent the creative gifts of fantasy and imagination? In your home or classroom, intentionally model one of these joyful activities (or perhaps this list brings to mind another). Ask children what kinds of celebration they enjoy. For the next seven days, use one of your choices and one of your children's choices to praise and thank God for your family, friends, classmates, health, and security. As you move into your third or fourth day, you may wish to expand your celebrations to thank God for Jesus, for His creation, your neighborhood, your country, your town, and so forth. Reflect and talk with children about your enjoyment and sense of joy and their enjoyment and sense of joy.

Every day find a way to tell your family and friends you love them. So often we assume they know. You might "shout" out as they go out the door, "I love you!" Encourage them to "shout" out "I love you" to one another in spontaneous moments. Be creative when you are serving children in a classroom, music, or sport environment to encourage them to "shout" their love and care for each other. Daily invite your children into your celebration. Remember, example and model are the most effective ways to form a spiritual practice in children.

Teaching Tip:

Example and model are the most effective ways to form a spiritual practice in children.

Celebrate the ordinary. At a meal, have dessert first. Or ask people to dress up for dinner. Suggest the dress be fancy on the top and "whatever" on the bottom. In one family who practiced this idea, the dad would show up in a tuxedo top and Bermuda shorts. His dress brought peals of laughter.

Celebrate maintenance. Young children love to help. Make a game out of collecting trash on trash day by giving each child a trash bag. The winner of the game is the one who collects the trash from his or her room (or other designated areas) the quickest. I often played this game with my children on Saturday mornings. The sooner we accomplished our maintenance tasks, the sooner we could move on with the play event for the day (picnic, movie, bike ride, etc.)

Most children like to celebrate anything. My friend tells me that her daughter, Mia, often asks to do something because "today's a special day, Mommy." My friend responds, "It is the only *today* we will ever have!" So they go to the library, make a smoothie, stop everything to snuggle, or whatever it is that the daughter finds fun to do.

Read stories or see movies with children that encourage laughter. Try the movie "What about Bob?" or the books *Alexander and the Terrible, Horrible, No Good, Very Bad Day* and *Ira Sleeps Over.* The Dr. Seuss tongue-twister books always bring laughter.

Read books about people who lived through difficult times and yet were able to celebrate. *The Five Little Peppers and How They Grew* is one example. *Runaway Slave* and *Ordeal in Cambodia* are other examples. Include some-real life stories such as Corrie ten Boom's about her time in the concentration camps. The book *The Heavenly Man* is the remarkable true story of a Chinese Christian, Brother Yun. Label how the characters in these stories celebrated life even in very difficult circumstances.

Ways For You To Practice And Model Celebration

Reflect: Every moment has the potential to be celebrated by our attitudes and actions. When was the last time you celebrated shopping at the grocery store? (That might have been to rejoice that you had the finances to purchase your needs and perhaps your wants.) How might you celebrate the tasks of laundry or paying bills?

Respond: List the areas in your life that seem to be drudgery, and ask God to give you ideas of how to celebrate them. Celebrate the ideas! You might try dancing or shouting your joy.

Activities And Guided Conversations For Children

Sing

Search for and sing songs with children to celebrate all kinds of events.

Guided Conversation

"It snowed last night. What were some of your thoughts, ideas, and adventures as you traveled to school (or piano lesson, sport event, woke up, saw the snow, etc.)?

"I like to celebrate a snowstorm with the simple song, 'It snowed last night, it snowed last night, the Sky Bears had a pillow fight, they tore up every cloud in sight and tossed them down as feathers light, oh, it snowed last night, it snowed last night.' (If you don't know the tune, make one up. Use your imagination.) Sing it with me."

Children enjoy songs that repeat words. One such celebration song that is based on Psalm 118 goes like this:

This is the day, this is the day
That the Lord has made, that the Lord has made;
We will rejoice, we will rejoice,
And be glad in it, and be glad in it.
This is the day that the Lord has made,
We will rejoice and be glad in it.

This is the day, this is the day
That the Lord has made.[7]

A couple of other songs you may enjoy are Psalm 8:1–3 "How Majestic Is Your Name" and Philippians 2:11 "He Is Lord."

Act Out

Create unexpected celebration events. On a cloudy, dreary, rainy, or snowy day, encourage children to create a warm, sunny environment in their classroom or at home. Provide or ask them to bring sandals, flip flops, shorts, and short-sleeves tee shirts.

Guided Conversation

"What is it like outside today? (Cloudy, dreary, rainy, snowy.) How could we imagine that we are on a beach? (Allow ideas.) What clothes could you need to wear on the beach? (Allow ideas.)

"Acting out a sunny day at the beach gives us the opportunity to create a time to celebrate the joy of life with each other. Let's put on our beach items and pretend we are having a celebration on the beach."

NOTE: You may also celebrate "un-birthdays" by reading the story "Alice in Wonderland" and singing the un-birthday song.

What About Celebration?

Provide a way to involve children with making a list of ordinary events.

Guided Conversation

"Let's think and talk about the practice of celebration. Where in your life might you need some celebration to bring joy to a task or responsibility? Wait. We need a recorder. Who would like to record our ideas on (notebook paper, chalkboard, chart paper, PowerPoint, etc.)? (Choose a recorder, and allow time for ideas to be given and recorded.)

"Some other ordinary events might include (name only those not already recorded):

- The beginning or ending of school
- A family vacation away from home
- A trip to the grocery store
- A trip to purchase new clothes
- Doing the laundry
- Doing yard work
- Setting the table
- Taking a walk

"What is a way we can choose one of our ideas for a celebration? (Allow ideas. One way may be to write events on slips of paper and draw one out.)

Now that we have made the choice, what are some ways we may bring celebration to this event?" (Allow ideas. Sing, dance, create a drama, make posters, plan a celebration, etc.)

APPENDIX

Appendix A

A Framework for How Children Think and Learn

Like an open book, you watched me grow from conception to birth;
all the stages of my life were spread out before you, the days of my
life all prepared before I'd even lived one day.

Psalm 139:16, MSG

As you explore how to help children live out the twelve spiritual disciplines presented in this book, it is important to have a firm grasp on some foundational concepts about children.

The illustration that follows shows five areas of child development: intellectual, physical, emotional, social, and spiritual. Take a moment to jot down what you understand about each area. With which area are you the most familiar? With which are you least familiar? Why?

AREAS OF DEVELOPMENT

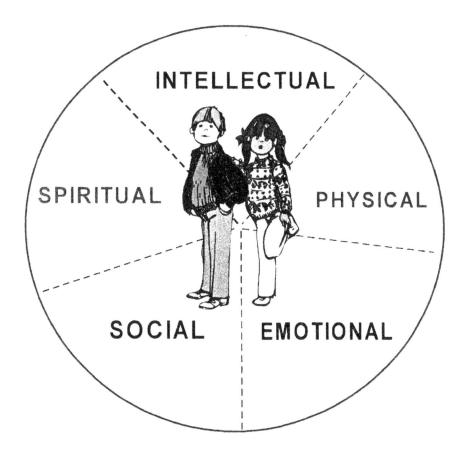

Often those who guide children touch on lightly or skip over the area of spiritual development. Since spiritual development is less tangible than physical development, there may be hesitancy for lack of understanding on how to create concrete learning experiences for abstract ideas. Or, perhaps spiritual development is touched on lightly or skipped over entirely because parents, teachers, and other adults are not fully aware of their own spiritual development or have not experienced intentional spiritual disciplines in their life.

The development of the spiritual area needs to be as intentional as the development of the intellectual, physical, social, and emotional areas. Are you beginning to see your challenges in guiding children to learn about and practice spiritual disciplines?

All areas of children's development affect and interact with one another. The spiritual development of children, however, is affected most directly by their stage of intellectual development. Since children's intellectual development is in what educators label as the concrete stage, *concrete experiences* form the basic structure of early childhood and children's thinking. Concrete experiences are those that allow children to use their five senses of touch, taste, sight, sound, and smell to assimilate concepts.

Most adults, in contrast to children, are able to do abstract thinking. *Abstract thinking* is thinking about ideas and concepts that cannot be experience with the five senses. It is the ability to think about relationships and symbolism, to formulate hypotheses, and to consider possibilities and abstractions such as forgiveness.

Previous studies about children's intellectual development concluded that the ability to think abstractly begins around the age of eleven or twelve. Recent studies, however, show that abstract thinking does not begin until age thirteen and in many teens much later. The ability to think abstractly does not suddenly appear at age thirteen. Those who are literal learners beyond the age of thirteen may always be limited to concrete thinking. As people who guide children in their spiritual formation, we have the responsibility to communicate the image and ideas of God in ways that are concrete and free of abstractions and symbolism, which confuse and give destructive ideas and images. In doing so, we offer children the opportunity to think and talk about God and His ways.

"The single most important thing in our minds is our idea of God," says Dallas Willard. "The process of spiritual formation in Christ is one of progressively replacing our destructive images and ideas with the images and ideas that filled the mind of Jesus Himself."[1] It is so important for us, then, at the earliest ages, to present children with images and ideas of God that accurately portray the compassionate, forgiving, God of integrity that He is.

Here are six challenges related to how children think and learn for you to keep in mind as you model and guide children to live out spiritual disciplines and build lifelong patterns and habits that grow their life with God.

Challenge One: Children's Limited Thinking

Children's thinking is limited by their perspective and life experience. Often when we talk with children about who God is, we talk about God as "our Father." We want to communicate that God's love never changes, that He consistently forgives us, that He is always there for us, and that He desires to have an intimate relationship with us.

A problem occurs when we talk only about God in this way to a child whose biological father is abusive, alcoholic, neglectful, or absent. Because of this child's limited life experience, his or her perspective of "father" is different (even opposite) from what we are trying to communicate about God.

Children need multiple concrete images and ideas about God in order to establish the relationship with God that Jesus spoke of and lived out. It is important to find some concrete realities that enlarge their ideas and thoughts about God besides His role as Father. The need is for ideas and images that are concrete and can be experienced with the five senses. The task is to form true perspectives about God for the child. Images might be a rainbow, the sun, stars, or beautiful trees covered with snow. Form an idea by asking, "What does a rainbow tell us about God?" and then connect the image and idea to the child with the comment, "God creates beautifully and wonderfully. He created you the same way. His rainbow tells us that God is with us here and now."

Challenge Two: Children's Focus On Non-Essentials

Not only is children's thinking limited by their perspective and life experience, but they also have a tendency to focus attention on secondary, or non-essential, aspects. Here's an example. A teacher is telling the story of Jesus being arrested by soldiers. The teacher mentions that the soldiers have swords. Caleb interrupts and begins talking about the new toy sword he received for his birthday. The child has fastened his attention on the secondary, or non-essential, part of the story that is familiar and important to him.

A perceptive adult might respond by guiding the conversation. "Caleb, I can tell how excited you are about your new toy sword. You may imagine that you have your sword here with you while you listen to what happened to the people in this Bible story." In this instance, the use of guided conversation helps the child refocus. It also helps the other children turn their thoughts back to the story.

Challenge Three: Meaningless Answers

Related to children's inability to focus on the significant portions of a situation is the ease with which children can give correct answers that are, in fact, meaningless to them. For instance, upon hearing a story of a woman who forgave her a child for telling a lie, a group of children was asked, "Why wasn't the woman angry and wanting to punish the child for doing wrong instead of being kind and forgiving?" One child replied, "Because the child said she was sorry, so the woman had to forgive her."

Did this child understand the abstract concept of the virtue of forgiveness, or did the child merely repeat something he or she had heard, that saying "I'm sorry" is the "right" answer? What would you say to this child if you were the storyteller?

A wise adult might respond by beginning with the part of forgiveness a child is most familiar with: "Forgiveness is more than saying 'I'm sorry.' Forgiveness begins when you agree with God that what you thought, said, or did is something God does not want people to think, say, or do." The adult can then say, "Forgiveness includes telling the person you hurt that what you thought, said, or did is wrong. Forgiveness also includes giving and receiving kindness and love. God's book the Bible says,

'Make sure that nobody pays back wrong for wrong, but always try to be kind to each other and to everyone else' (1 Thessalonians 5:15)."

In this illustration we can see that children are able to repeat words that are expected of them by adults, give correct answers they have learned to give, and receive praise from adults, all the while not understanding what the words mean. By listening carefully to what children say and asking open-ended questions, we are able to guide children's understanding from mere repetition to meaningful interaction and communication.

Challenge Four: Correct Interpretation

Often a great deal of misunderstanding occurs in children's thinking because they incorrectly interpret abstract words to fit their concrete thinking. Some adults think these misunderstandings are humorous. And they are. But laughter may be perceived as belittling. These misinterpretations are in fact a clue that the children are thinking concretely. Here is an example.

Not long ago I was visiting a young child in her home. Her parents were so excited for me to hear that their five-year-old had memorized the twenty-third Psalm. After the child repeated all of the verses from memory, I asked, "What parts of these words do you like the most?" I don't really know," she responded, "but I don't want to lie down in a green pasture."

Now listen to this conversation and think about how you might respond. Five-year-old Justin is sitting in church. He keeps himself busy by singing and talking. His seven-year-old sister tells him to stop. Justin answers, "Why? Who's going to make me?" Justin's sister says, "See those men holding the bulletins? They are called 'hushers'."

As people who desire to guide children intentionally in their spiritual formation, we have the opportunity to listen carefully to what children say and then, with gentle kindness, lead them to the correct interpretation. A helpful response in this situation might be: "The name of the people holding bulletins is 'usher.' To usher means to help people by giving them a bulletin and perhaps finding them a place to sit. I can tell you are being observant and thinking, because the name usher sure sounds like 'husher'."

Challenge Five: Firsthand Experiences

Because children think concretely, firsthand experiences give them opportunities to use their five senses to gain understanding. When an adult wants a child to experience an abstract concept such as kindness, the adult needs to create or take advantage of a quality firsthand experience that demonstrates kindness. For example, nine-year-old Juanita's teacher or parent may take advantage of a time when she or he sees Juanita being kind to her friend Raul by saying, "Juanita, giving your book to Raul was a kind thing to do." Creating a firsthand experience might include asking a child to do something kind: "Carlos, would you please do me a kindness by holding the door open for me?"

Increasing the quantity and quality of firsthand experiences occurs as we make a habit to continuously watch for, label, and describe firsthand experiences. Take advantage of everyday opportunities. Notice the labeling in these sentences. "*Thank you for inviting* Tammy to sit next to you. The invitation was a *kind thing to do*." "Choosing to participate in just one sport activity this year shows that you are *practicing the important discipline of simplicity*." "Slowing down and allowing the older gentleman to enter the store first tells me you are *thinking of others. You are becoming a compassionate person*."

Challenge Six: Physical Experiences

Children's intellectual development and spiritual development require physical experiences and objects to manipulate. An abstract idea such as trust, for example, needs to be recast in physical experiences to enable children to attach meaning to the abstract concept.

Creating a physical experience for trust may be as simple as having children experience a trust walk. In a trust walk, children are paired. One child is blindfolded, and the other is not. The blindfolded child is led safely around simple objects by the other child. The blindfolded child experiences trust, while the other child experiences being a trustworthy guide. In conversation afterwards, the children may be asked to describe what attitude was needed to trust and what attitude was needed to be trustworthy.

To increase children's attention span, provide a squishy ball to hold and squeeze while listening to a story or waiting at a doctor's office or some other tedious place.

When we use these six challenges as a framework for guiding children in the spiritual disciplines, we allow children to explore and grow their spiritual life, their life with God, in the best and most personal way.

Appendix B

Guided Conversation

The importance of *guided conversation* cannot be overemphasized. Guided conversation makes possible the building of good relationships, the discovery of a child's knowledge, and opportunities to guide learners' beliefs, attitudes, and understanding. Guided conversation also enables affirming children's discernment about God's presence and direction.

Keep in mind that words have tremendous power. The words we use and the way we guide conversation greatly impact spiritual and character formation in children, their families, and communities.

Guided conversation makes it possible to explore openly and freely children's deepest questions about their personal lives, their families, their friends, their school, and their play experiences. In my years of serving children and facilitating the learning of others who serve children, I have found that some adults consider opening this conversation avenue a bit of a threat. Perhaps it is because they have come to believe that they must have all the answers to children's questions.

When you do not know how to answer a child's question, simply say, "I don't know the answer to your question. Let's begin to pray and research to find some information together. In order to offer children a fuller experience of life with God, it is our responsibility to draw out, in everyday, walk-around experiences, an understanding of God and God's desires for the people He created.

Guided conversation creates the opportunity to model spiritual disciplines and character virtues. Here are a few ideas, skills, and activities to enhance your use of guided conversation.

- Listen and discover what children think. This is essential. Expect to learn from them. Ask for clarification. Their ideas may be different from yours, and their experiences may differ from those you are suggesting. For instance, when in a discussion about what God might have us be and do for homeless people, one child shared a personal story about going shopping for a new outfit and seeing homeless men and women holding up signs by the highway exit requesting work or other help. She reported that her mother locked the doors of the car and kept driving.

A wise adult who hears this child's unspoken desire for guidance might respond, "What would you have thought or liked to do?" In this experience, some of the children's responses included that they thought holding up signs about being homeless was "stupid" and "a waste of rich people's time." Accepting these ideas does not mean you agree. Accepting makes it possible for children to tell what they really are thinking. A response might sound like, "That is one way to think about their reason for signs. Can you think of another?

- Ask questions one at a time. Children have difficulty with complex sentences or multiple questions at once. Say, "What would be a way to help people who are homeless?" instead of "What would be a way to help people who are homeless, and do you have an example of a time when you or you and your family helped the homeless?"

- Allow time for children to think. Ask, "Why would we desire to help those who are homeless?" and then wait for answers. Count to ten before you assume children are not able to answer.

- Reveal the source where truth and direction might be found. Say, "In God's book the Bible, we find words that tell us to care for those in need. Let's look for some of those words." Try Deuteronomy 15:4, "There should be no poor among you" or Psalm 82:3, "Defend the cause of the weak and fatherless; maintain the rights of the poor and oppressed." Be sure children understand that God is asking those who have to care for those who have not.

- Clarify the difference between fact and opinion. "Some of you said that you thought holding up signs about being homeless was 'stupid'. Let's see if that is a fact or an opinion. All those who have talked with homeless people about why they make these signs and what results they have from the signs, please raise your hands." After children see the response, say, "So is the comment about signs fact or opinion?"

- Clarify the difference between questions and statements. "It takes courage to be with people who are in need," says Carlos with some uncertainty in his voice. The wise adult may then respond, "Is your remark a question or a statement? If it is a question, you are letting me know that you want to know more about courage. If it is a statement, the answer is, it does take a lot of courage and guidance to be with people who are in need."

Appendix C

Spiritual Disciplines: Definitions for Children and Supporting Scriptures

Meditation—Child friendly words: thinking about God, listening, and hearing His voice.

Think over what I say, for the Lord will give you understanding in all things.
2 Timothy 2:7, *The RENOVARÉ Spiritual Formation Bible*, NRSV

My sheep listen to my voice; I know them, and they follow me.
John 10:27

Prayer—Child friendly words: talking with God, listening to God, and spending time with God.

We do not know how to pray as we should. But the Spirit himself speaks to God for us, even begs God for us. The Spirit speaks to God with deep feelings that words cannot explain.
Romans 8:26, ICB

Be joyful always; pray continually; give thanks in all circumstances, for this is God's will for you in Christ Jesus.
1 Thessalonians 5:16-18

Study—Child friendly words: read the Bible, observe, and be informed by God's words and ways.

Do not be conformed to this world, but be transformed by the renewing of your minds, so that you may discern what is the will of God—what is good and acceptable and perfect.
Romans 12:2, NRSV

Do not change yourselves to be like the people of this world. But be changed within by a new way of thinking. Then you will be able to decide what God wants for you. And you will be able to know what is good and pleasing to God and what is perfect.

Romans 12:2, ICB

Fasting—Child friendly words: let go and take on.

I humbled my soul with fasting.

Psalm 69:10, NRSV

I proclaimed a fast, so that we might humble ourselves before our God.

Ezra 8:21

Simplicity—Child friendly words: living a simpler life of joyful unconcern from wanting more and more.

Then Jesus said to them, "Be careful and guard against all kinds of greed. A man's life is not measured by the many things he owns."

Luke 12:15, ICB

Therefore I tell you, do not worry about your life, what you will eat or drink; or about your body, what you will wear. Is not life more important than food, and the body more important than clothes?

Matthew 6:26

Solitude—Child friendly words: spend time with God.

For God alone my soul waits in silence, from him comes my salvation.

Psalm 62:5, NRSV

Be still, and know that I am God.

Psalm 46:10

Submission—Child friendly words: giving love, care, and respect to God and others.

But he gives us all the more grace; therefore it says,
"God opposes the proud,
But gives grace to the humble."
Submit yourselves therefore to God.

James 4:6–7, NRSV

Do nothing out of selfish ambition or vain conceit, but in humility consider others better than yourselves.

Philippians 2:3

Submit to one another out of reverence for Christ.

Ephesians 5:21

Service—Child friendly words: become a servant to all.

Little children, let us love, not in word or speech, but in truth and action.

1 John 3:18, NRSV

Serve wholeheartedly, as if you were serving the Lord.

Ephesians 6:7

Confession—Child friendly words: telling the truth.

If we say that we have no sin, we are fooling ourselves, and the truth is not in us. But if we confess our sins, he will forgive our sins. We can trust God. He does what is right. He will make us clean from all the wrongs we have done.

1 John 1:8–9, ICB

Therefore confess your sins to each other and pray for each other so that you may be healed.

James 5:16

Worship—Child friendly words: to focus on God.

You are worthy, our Lord and God, to receive glory and honor and power, for you created all things, and by your will they were created and have their being.

Revelation 4:11

But the hour is coming, and is now here, when the true worshippers will worship the Father in Spirit and truth, for the Father seeks such as these to worship him.

John 4:23, NRSV

Guidance—Child friendly words: search for and discern God's presence and direction.

For this God is our God forever and ever; he will be our guide even to the end.

Psalm 48:14

Make plans by seeking advice.

Proverbs 20:18

Whether you turn to the right or to the left, your ears will hear a voice behind you, saying, "This is the way; walk in it."

Isaiah 30:21

Celebration—Child friendly words: having joy and delight.

If you obey my commands, you will remain in my love, just as I have obeyed my Father's commands and remain in his love. I have told you this so that my joy may be in you and that your joy may be complete.

John 15:10–11

Delight yourself in the LORD and he will give you the desires of your heart.

Psalm 37:4

Direct me in the path of your commands, for there I find delight.

Psalm 119:35

Appendix D

Character Virtues and Vices

Character is a collection of virtues and vices. The word *virtue* means good. I have chosen to use the word *virtue* to describe "constructive character" and the word *vice* to describe "destructive character." Everyone receives character formation, just as everyone receives an education. The task is to be intentional in the formation of godly constructive character virtues in our children in tandem with the practice of spiritual disciplines.

Eight virtues, which I have labeled *foundation virtues*, were identified through extensive study of God's basic character qualities. Each foundation virtue has an opposite, or vice. Constructive virtues are antidotes to destructive vices.

CHARACTER VIRTUES	CHARACTER VICES
Compassion	Indifference
Forgiveness	Vengeance
Integrity	Dishonesty, Promise Breaking
Respect	Disdain (Scorn, Contempt)
Responsibility	Irresponsibility, Unwillingness to Commit
Initiative	Slothfulness, Laziness
Cooperation	Dissension, Opposition
Perseverance	Giving Up

After identifying these foundation virtues, other virtues were identified that may be formed in tandem with the each foundation virtue. I have labeled these virtues *family virtues*. Family virtues develop and grow from the foundation virtues.

The foundation virtues are the larger concepts. For example, the foundation virtue of integrity includes truth, honesty, promise keeping, discernment, justice, and commitment, among others. Each family virtue is a smaller concept but an integral part of the foundation virtue.

Foundation Virtues and Family Virtues

Foundation virtues are listed in bold print with their family virtues listed below. These virtues are based on God's character.

COMPASSION

Love, Care, Kindness,
Self-Esteem, Self-Control,
Obedience, Promise Keeping,
Gentleness, Empathy, Trust,
Generosity, Sacrifice, Courage,
Justice

FORGIVENESS

Humility, Joy, Peace,
Mercy, Grace, Love,
Thankfulness, Gratitude,
Hope, Trust, Tenderness,
Justice

INTEGRITY

Truth, Honesty, Discernment,
Faithfulness, Trust, Wisdom,
Promise Keeping, Sincerity,
Commitment, Justice

RESPECT

Obedience, Patience,
Loyalty, Tolerance,
Courtesy, Honor, Encouragement

RESPONSIBILITY

Self-Discipline,
Self-Control, Dependability,
Obedience, Trust, Patience

INITIATIVE

Generosity, Courage,
Motivation, Boldness

COOPERATION

Authority, Generosity,
Goodness, Kindness, Humor

PERSEVERANCE

Endurance, Diligence,
Dependability, Loyalty,
Courage, Hope, Patience

Foundation Virtues: Definitions and Benefits to Society

<u>Compassion</u>
Definition: Compassion is sympathy for someone else's suffering or misfortune, together with the desire to help, and appropriate action for his or her benefit.

Benefits to society: All people want and need compassion. When people build relationships on compassion rather than power, they act to give to each other the best they have. Compassion allows people to bear all things, believe all things, hope all things, and endure all things.

Scripture basis: "Jesus called his disciples to him and said, 'I have compassion for these people; they have already been with me three days and have nothing to eat. I do not want to send them away hungry, or they may collapse on the way'" (Matthew 15:32). In this Scripture, we see that Jesus lived out the private, inward compassion of His Father.

"[The Lord] crowns you with love and compassion" (Psalm 103:4).

Forgiveness
Definition: Forgiveness means to no longer blame or be angry with someone who has hurt or wronged you, including yourself. Forgiveness is to pardon or excuse a wrong thought, word, attitude, or action without condition.

Benefits to society: When people practice forgiveness in the community, they break the cycle of revenge. When a person experiences forgiveness, he or she is freed from guilt and attitudes of failure. When people feel they have failed, they lose their productivity. When people receive forgiveness, they regain their motivation to contribute to society.

Scripture basis: "Love your enemies, do good to them… and you will be sons of the Most High, because he is kind to the ungrateful and wicked" (Luke 6:35). Notice that this Scripture points to an intimate connection between compassion and forgiveness.

"If you forgive others their trespasses, your heavenly Father will also forgive you" (Matthew 6:14, NRSV).

"Bear with each other and forgive whatever grievances you may have against one another. Forgive as the Lord forgave you" (Colossians 3:13).

Integrity
Definition: Integrity is strength and firmness of character that results in consistent sincerity and honesty. People of integrity keep their word.

Benefits to society: Many systems of law and justice are based upon the Bible. These teachings provide an absolute standard for integrity so that society can determine whether the action of an individual is acceptable or not. An absolute standard keeps corrupt leaders from making one law for the people and another law for themselves. As people act with integrity, integrity is infused into society, bringing maximum value to the law.

Scripture basis: "In everything…show integrity, seriousness and soundness of speech" (Titus 2:7–8).

Respect
Definition: Respect is showing honor to people by listening, being courteous and polite, and demonstrating manners. It includes self-respect, the avoidance of excessive self-criticism, and respect for order and authority.

Benefits to society: People promote respect by considering others as important as themselves. Respect is an outcome of demonstrating honor to people. The result is a society that demonstrates respect for order and authority.

Scripture basis: "Each of you must respect his mother and father" (Leviticus 19:3a). "Rise in the presence of the aged, show respect for the elderly and revere your God. I am the LORD" (Leviticus 19:32).

Responsibility
Definition: Responsibility is the personal, individual acceptance that every human being is accountable for his or her behavior, including thoughts, choices, decisions, speech, and actions.

Benefits to society: Individuals, families, and social groups win when each carries its share of responsibility. When a society is made up of responsible citizens, it is possible to focus on ways to solve problems through logical consequence, moral character, conscience, and right and wrong.

Scripture basis: "Each person must be responsible for himself" (Galatians 6:5, ICB).

Initiative
Definition: Initiative is choosing to take the first step in thinking, doing, or learning. It includes being responsible for follow-through. Initiative is demonstrating responsible thoughts and actions without being prompted or without being influenced by limited choices.

Benefits to society: Initiative is grounded in first steps and follow-through. Initiative results in the ability to create, to solve problems, and to continue what is begun until it is completed. People who initiate are risk takers and are character driven. They act without prompting and take the first steps in resolving disputes. These behaviors, attitudes, and conduct result in a society of responsible citizens with positive, productive work ethics; constructive attitudes toward others; and motivation to provide solutions.

Scripture basis: "I can do all things through Christ because he gives me strength" (Philippians 4:13, ICB).

Cooperation

Definition: Cooperation is working together to reach a common goal. A cooperative person is willing to work with others in an effort to accomplish something that cannot be achieved by a single person. Cooperation is sharing skills, energy, talents, respect, and responsibility with others.

Benefits to society: The mutual good of society is more likely to be attained when people work, play, and study cooperatively. No one person is able to accomplish all that is needed for a society. By working together, people can strive collectively to educate their young, make medical care possible, maintain law and order, make housing and food available, provide products and services, and temper the worst aspects of competition.

Scripture basis: "Two people are better than one. They get more done by working together" (Ecclesiastes 4:9, ICB).

Perseverance

Definition: Perseverance is continual, steady effort made to fulfill some purpose, goal, task, or commitment. It means persistence in spite of difficulties, opposition, or discouragement. Perseverance is the refusal to give up when things are difficult. It is the habit of following through and finishing what was started.

Benefits to society: When individuals practice perseverance, they contribute to society the ability to see a task or commitment through to completion, and to keep doing right regardless of problems or persecution. The ability to persevere is foundational for education, employment, religion, relationships, leadership, and marriage.

Scripture basis: "The testing of your faith develops perseverance. Perseverance must finish its work so that you may be mature and complete, not lacking anything" (James 1:3-4).

Appendix E

A Prayer Guide for Children to Invite Jesus into Their Life

How early in life is it possible for children to be aware of life with God? To talk to and hear God's voice? To respond to the Holy Spirit's prompting to invite Jesus into their life?

Much of the disagreement on this question seems to be focused on the age or stage of development at which children are considered to be accountable for their decisions and actions. Perhaps it is the mental and emotional age of a child and the way in which that child's spiritual life is being developed rather than the chronological age of the child that is a determining factor. A larger factor, however, is the nature of the child's community, which is determined by the character and spiritual life of the key influencers in the child's life.

A community striving to have a life with God creates an atmosphere and environment where children touch, taste, smell, see, and hear the "with-God life." A community striving to have a life with God becomes a place where children grow in their understanding of a relationship with Jesus, His Father God, and the Holy Spirit as their helper and guide. It becomes a place where children observe parents, relatives, teacher, coaches, and others reading God's book the Bible and talking with God.

Such a community is a place where children may take part in asking and answering questions about how God comes to us. It is a place where they can learn by example and guidance to trust and obey God and be people of compassion, forgiveness, and integrity.

The goal for those who lead children and families in these communities is spiritual and character formation into the likeness of Christ. The purpose of all "with-God life" communities is to have children understand that God is with them and He always desires to love and care for them and in return for them to love God. These communities are also responsible to guide children to a time when they make a personal choice to invite God to not only be with them but to live in them.

Rather than just viewing a "salvation moment" as the first and foremost experience, it is important for us as children's advocates to understand and focus attention on each of these parts of the big picture:

- Preparation of children to make a decision for Christ.
- Guidance of children without pressure to invite Jesus into their life.
- Guidance in a "with-God life" that brings continued spiritual formation.

When children ask for guidance in how to pray to invite Jesus into their life, it helps for us to ask the concrete question, "Would you like to ask Jesus to be with you and in you now?" This carefully worded question allows children to say yes, no, or "I would like to wait awhile." You may respond to a "no" statement or an "I would like to wait" statement by saying, "When you are ready to ask Jesus to be with you and in you, just let me know, and I will enjoy praying with you."

When children say yes, guide them to talk to God using their own words or a prayer like this:

Dear God, I believe Jesus is Your Son. Thank You that Jesus died on the cross for the wrong things I have thought, said, or done. Please forgive me for doing wrong. I ask that Jesus will be with me and in me always. Thank You for always being with me. Help me be more and more like You. Thank You for answering this prayer.

A booklet I have written for guiding children as they explore inviting Jesus into their life is titled "The Greatest Promise." The booklet may be ordered from www. characterchoice.org or www. Jesusfilmstore.com.

Source Notes

INTRODUCTION

1 George Barna, *Transforming Children Into Spiritual Champions* (Ventura, CA: Regal, 2003), 28.
2 Ibid., 41.
3 Bishop Dr. Sterling Lands II, Presiding Bishop of the Family Life International Fellowship, Senior Pastor of the Greater Calvary Bible Church, Austin, TX.
4 Sterling Lands, II, *The Main Ingredient* (Austin, TX: Greater Calvary Publishing, 2002), 79.

CHAPTER 1

1 Richard Foster, *Celebration of Discipline* (San Francisco: HarperCollins, 1998), 17.
2 Eugene H. Peterson, *The Jesus Way* (Grand Rapids: Wm. B. Eerdmans Publishing Co., 2007), 28.
3 Marti Watson and Valerie Hess, *Habits of a Child's Heart* (Colorado Springs, CO: NavPress, 2004), 29.

CHAPTER 2

1 Richard J. Foster, *Prayer: Finding the Heart's True Home* (San Francisco: HarperSanFrancisco, 1992), 8.
2 CD "It Takes Love" is available at http://characterchoice.org.
3 Frank C. Laubach, *Learning the Vocabulary of God* (Nashville: Upper Room, 1956), 22–23.

CHAPTER 3

1 Alan Andrews, Ed., *The Kingdom Life: A Practical Theology of Discipleship and Spiritual Formation* (Colorado Springs, CO: NavPress, 2010), 64.

2 Ibid., 67.
3 Dallas Willard, *Renovation of the Heart* (Colorado Springs, CO: NavPress, 2002), 248.

CHAPTER 4

1 Richard J. Foster, *Celebration of Discipline* (New York, NY: Harper San Francisco, 1998), 56.
2 Valerie E. Hess and Marti Watson Garlett, *Habits of a Child's Heart* (Colorado Springs, CO: NavPress, 2004), 57-63.

CHAPTER 5

1 Richard Foster, *Celebration of Discipline* (San Francisco: HarperSanFrancisco, 1998), 82.
2 David Elkind, *Hurried Child*, 3d ed. (Cambridge, Mass: Perseus Publishing, 2001), *xv.*

CHAPTER 6

1 Jan Johnson, *When the Soul Listens* (Colorado Springs, CO: NavPress, 1999), 80.
2 Vivian L. Houk, *Parenting by Developmental Design* (Eugene, OR: Resource Publications, 2010), 115.

CHAPTER 7

1 Richard Foster, *Celebration of Discipline* (San Francisco: HarperCollins, 1998), 115.
2 See Matthew 25:40.
3 Henri J.M. Nouwen, *In the Name of Jesus* (New York, NY: Crossroad Publishing Company, 1989), 63.
4 Valerie E. Hess and Marti Watson Garlett, *Habits of a Child's Heart* (Colorado Springs, CO: NavPress, 2004), 122.

CHAPTER 8

1 Richard J. Foster and Julia L. Roller, *A Year With God: Living Out the Spiritual Disciplines* (New York: HarperCollins, 2008), 106.
2 Richard Foster, *Celebration of Discipline* (San Francisco: HarperCollins, 1998), 130.

3 William Law, *A Serious Call to a Devout and Holy Life* (Nashville: Upper Room Press, 1952), 26.

4 Vernie Schorr, *Compass: A Guide for Character and Spiritual Formation in Children* (Erie, CO: Character Choice, 2008), 30.

5 Ibid., 42.

CHAPTER 9

1 Valerie Hess, *Spiritual Disciplines Devotional* (Downers Grove, IL: InterVarsity Press, 2007), 202.

2 Used by permission. From "It Takes Love" music CD available through Character Choice, www.characterchoice.org.

CHAPTER 10

1 Richard J. Foster and Julia L. Roller, *A Year with God: Living Out the Spiritual Disciplines* (New York: HarperOne, 2009), Day 86.

2 Eugene H. Peterson, *A Long Obedience in the Same Direction* (Downers Grove, IL: InterVarsity Press, 2000), 56.

3 Kathleen Chapman, *Teaching Kids Authentic Worship* (Grand Rapids, MI: Baker Books, 2004), 34.

4 *Sing to the Lord Praise Book* (Camdenton, MO: G/L Publications), #77.

5 Chapman, *Teaching Kids Authentic Worship,* 91.

6 Richard Foster, *Celebration of Discipline* (San Francisco: HarperCollins, 1998), 163–164.

7 Chapman, *Teaching Kids Authentic Worship*, 18.

8 *Jesus, You Are Holy,* Words and Music by Ed Steele (Broadman Press (SESAC), Nashville, TN, 1999).

CHAPTER 11

1 Ruth Haley Barton, *Sacred Rhythms* (Downers Grove, IL: InterVarsity Press, 2006), 111.

CHAPTER 12

1 *The RENOVARÉ Spiritual Formation Bible* (San Francisco: HarperCollins, 2005), 513.

2 Valerie Hess, *Habits of a Child's Heart* (Colorado Springs: NavPress, 2004), 182.

3 Richard Foster, *Celebration of Discipline* (San Francisco: HarperCollins, 1998), 193.

4 Ibid., 196.

5 *Children's Ministry Magazine* Vol. 20, No. 6 (January/February 2011): 32.

6 Dallas Willard, *The Spirit of the Disciplines* (San Francisco: Harper & Row, 1988), 179.

7 *Let's Sing,* Scripture Press Publication, Inc. Wheaton, Illinois, second printing, 1986, 8.

APPENDIX

1 Alan Andrews, *The Kingdom Life: A Practical Theology of Discipleship and Spiritual Formation* (Colorado Springs: NavPress, 2010), 50. Quote taken from chapter written by Dallas Willard.

Index